Expanding the Canon:
Bridges to Understanding

Articles from
English Journal, 1987–89

Selected by
Faith Z. Schullstrom

National Council of Teachers of English
1111 Kenyon Road, Urbana, Illinois 61801

Staff Editor: Tim Bryant

Cover Design: Michael J. Getz

Interior Design: Tom Kovacs for TGK Design

NCTE Stock Number 16477-3020

It is the policy of NCTE in its journals and other publications to provide a forum for the open discussion of ideas concerning the content and the teaching of English and the language arts. Publicity accorded to any particular point of view does not imply endorsement by the Executive Committee, the Board of Directors, or the membership at large, except in announcements of policy, where such endorsement is clearly specified.

Library of Congress Cataloging-in-Publication Data
Expanding the canon : bridges to understanding : articles from
    English journal, 1987–89 / selected by Faith Z. Schullstrom.
        p.   cm.
      ISBN 0-8141-1647-7
        1. American literature—Study and teaching (Secondary) 2. English
    literature—Study and teaching (Secondary) 3. Canon (Literature)
    I. Schullstrom, Faith Z. II. National Council of Teachers of English.
    III. English journal.
    PS41.E97   1991
    807'.1'273—dc20   90-23543
                                                                      CIP

Contents

Preface

Expanding the Canon: Bridges to Understanding is a collection of articles originally printed in *English Journal*, the secondary section membership journal of the National Council of Teachers of English (NCTE). The articles selected for this book tap a rich vein of multicultural literature, including works by African Americans, Native Americans, women, and authors from outside of North America and Europe. The selections span many genres, including Young Adult Novels, Popular Fiction, Science Fiction, and Classical Fiction. Each article presents practical suggestions for incorporating these works into the secondary classroom, thus broadening the cultural perspective of students and teachers alike.

This book also serves as an excellent introduction to the professional resources available to NCTE members. The Council promotes the development of literacy through the learning and teaching of English and the related arts and sciences of language. Membership is available to teachers and administrators at all levels, and to all others who are interested in the promotion of literacy through the teaching of English and the language arts. For membership information, write to: NCTE, 1111 Kenyon Road, Urbana, IL 61801.

1 YA Novels in the AP Classroom: Crutcher Meets Camus

Patricia Spencer

"Our next assignment, *No Exit*, it's not more of the same philosophy, is it?" a seventeen-year-old senior queries disgustedly.

"Why do you ask?"

"I just can't get involved, but we have to read another, huh?" Lethargically, she picks up the Jean-Paul Sartre play, exiting as a second group of bright, college-bound, advanced-placement students enter.

Another discussion. Dutiful analysis. Insightful, detached comments. Probing, I search to help students find significance in an AP English unit on philosophy in literature. Instead, characters like Meursault, Marie, Estelle, Garcin, and Inez appear as alien as the philosophy of estrangement. As this class picks up copies of *No Exit*, an aloof athlete grabs a book from the shelf below. "Why don't we read something contemporary?" He holds up a copy of Chris Crutcher's *Running Loose*. Laughing, he eyes the cover kiss and does a dramatic reading of the title kicker: "For Louie the only way to make it is his way."

I pause: it's worth a try.

"Forget *No Exit* tonight. Take a copy of *Running Loose* and enjoy."

Discovering the existential elements and heroes in modern adolescent literature has been a needed addition to an advanced-placement English course. Naturally, the "classics" are not abandoned (Meursault goes on trial annually), but now the unit has the vitality of teenage existentialists who, even in the last quarter of the twentieth century, are searching for individuality and identity, who pose questions, find conundrums, and validate insecurities casually disguised by designer jeans, lip gloss, or football jerseys.

Adolescent literature offers both novels and short stories with existential elements. The novels *The Crazy Horse Electric Game* (1987, New York: Dell) and *Running Loose* (1983, New York: Dell) by Chris Crutcher contain male protagonists who face personal adversity: in

1

Crazy Horse, Willie Weaver, an athlete crippled in a freak water-skiing accident, struggles for physical and emotional recovery: in *Running Loose*, Louie Banks, a football player ostracized by school and community when he opposes an unethical coach, deals with the sudden death of his girlfriend. Norma Howe's *God, the Universe and Hot Fudge Sundaes* (1984, Boston: Houghton) portrays Alfie, a gifted adolescent female, coping with her sister's death, parents' divorce, and her own religious doubts. All three novels illustrate various aspects of that nebulous philosophy explored by Jean-Paul Sartre:

> Man can count on no one but himself: he is alone, abandoned on earth in the midst of his infinite responsibilities, without help, with no other aim than the one he sets himself, with no other destiny than the one he forges for himself on this earth. (1964, "Sartre and Existentialism," *Life* 6 Nov.: 86–112, [87])

Sartre's words reflect basic characteristics of the literary existential world and hero.

Alienation

After the accident, seemingly abandoned in his bitterness by girlfriend, parents, and teammates, Willie Weaver in *Crazy Horse* is indeed alone. The courageous bus trip from Idaho to Oakland separates him from those on whom he might depend. Physically disabled and emotionally crushed, Willie appears an alien in an unfamiliar world; the basketball court and baseball diamond no longer welcome him. His own body is foreign to him: "His gait is uneven; right side jogging, left side following—dragging. . . . Nothing about it feels athletic, nothing pleasing" (54).

In a reading journal, a student comments, "As a wrestler, I know what it means to be in tune with my body. I feel Willie's pain; I live in fear of injury. I would lose my whole identity."

Estrangement invades the life of Louie Banks in *Running Loose* when he takes a stand against his football coach and principal. Unwilling to play dirty ball, Louie is labeled a "nigger lover" and "wussy" and loses his position on the team and the opportunity to participate in any team sports. Quick to point out a less obvious alienation, another student mentions how alone Louie is in personal mourning: surely others mourn Becky, but grief is personal, as Louie demonstrates in his outburst at the funeral:

> He [God] doesn't move in strange and mysterious ways. He doesn't move at all! He sits up there on his fat butt and lets guys like you

[the minister] earn a living making excuses for all the rotten things
that happen. Or maybe He does something low-down every once in
a while so He can get a bunch of us together, scared and on our
knees. Hell with Him! (136–37)

Students also note the general air of individuality in Crutcher's
characterization of Louie: "he doesn't follow the crowd in anything."

In *God, the Universe and Hot Fudge Sundaes*, Alfie, too, is alone
after Francie's death: the nurse leaves, Alfie's father moves out, and
her mother, a born-again Christian with fundamentalist beliefs, re-
treats to a Bible-study group. Alone, Alfie tackles some of the questions
that plagued both Socrates and Sartre, weighing the forces of faith
and reason.

Chaos

"Just when I start believing I have some control, that I can take charge,
instead of my parents running my life, I start to see that I really have no
control," concludes one student, the day following the schoolyard
slaughter in Stockton, California. In his reading-journal entry, he
explores Louie Banks's situation: "The randomness of events is evident.
Without reason or justification, Becky dies. Funny word: accident. Life
is an accident of chance Louie must face. Me, too." Similarly, Willie
Weaver in *Crazy Horse* loses his physical identity in a freak water-skiing
episode, pushing himself too far, expecting superhuman powers which
do not rescue him. One moment he's the baseball champion, later the
crippled ex-athlete. The existential premise of a universe in chaos raises
the question of external control: is there a God who allows this to
happen? In *Hot Fudge* Alfie struggles: "I'm having trouble trying to
figure out why an all-powerful God would create a person like Francie
just to make her suffer and die" (142). Later, she drifts "into that strange
interlude between wakefulness and sleep," trying to picture Francie in
an afterlife: "She couldn't be alive and here one minute, and then just
gone forever, the next" (147). During an unsuccessful trip to retrieve a
lost crucifix in the family's former home, Alfie witnesses her lack of
control. A new condominium stands where she'd hoped to find the cross
in a closet drawer of an older home: the permanently misplaced crucifix
works as a symbol of Alfie's lost beliefs.

A student journal entry on *Running Loose* picks up this idea: "Louie
tries to pray about Becky's death, but he feels abandoned. Maybe no
answer is an answer, but Louie doesn't accept it." Toward the end of
chapter 12, Louie says,

> If there's a good reason, then you owe me an explanation, so let's
> have it. . . . After I figured I'd given Lord God Almighty plenty of
> time to answer and He didn't, I walked over to the pickup and
> dragged my granddad's old double-bitted ax out of the bed and
> came back and brought that tree to the ground. . . . It must have
> taken me forty-five minutes, but I stood there blasting away and
> screaming, "Is this yours? How do you like it?" (127)

The absurdity of death prompts brutal responses from these adolescent
philosophers.

Commitment

All of this would be unbearably depressing if it were not for the idea of
the existential choice: to find individual meaning in this chaos. In
discussion, students describe Louie's existential engagement: "Right
from the start, Louie seems able to forge his own path; his principles
come from within. Whether he's dealing with Boomer, Coach Led-
necky, or even Becky, he's firm, striving to make his own sense of the
situation." Another almost interrupts, "And take a look at how he
reaches, well, pretty much the depth of despair after Becky's death. He
could have continued sinking, but he attempts to put things together. I
really think he finds out more of who he is when he commits to track."

Students sharing ideas on *The Crazy Horse Electric Game* are soon
comparing Willie Weaver's situation to Meursault in Albert Camus's
The Stranger: "Neither character commits until he's imprisoned:
Meursault in actual confinement and Willie a prisoner in his own
disabled body." Another student extends the comparison:

> Or did you notice how the scene between Willie and his father on
> the racquetball court parallels *No Exit*? They are torturing each
> other and themselves in confinement. Willie doesn't start recovery
> until he breaks away, takes his own path toward meaning.

An advanced-placement student devours an adolescent novel in a
single evening; change of pace, ease, and interest level provide new
accessibility to the difficult, cold philosophy of existentialism. Although YA novels serve as better catalysts for extensive, in-depth
philosophical comparisons, young-adult short stories are viable alter-
natives when time or materials may be problematic. Lois Ruby's
"Justice," from *Arriving at a Place You Never Left* (1977, New York:
Dial) provides a rival for Meursault's cool, detached trial demeanor.
Jonah, fourteen, has murdered his father to prevent further abuse of a
younger brother; dispassionate composure, sensory detail, and tone

echo Camus. In "Trophy," from Barbara Girion's collection, *A Very Brief Season* (1984, New York: Scribner's), Stacey, a high-school student who has attended five schools in three years, lives on the fringe, an alien without involvement; indifferently she collects trophies of discarded relationships, which students compare to the Meursault-Marie affair.

Adolescent literature in an advanced-placement classroom connects classics to the present. Even those students who read Nietzsche on their own find relevance and pleasure in sharing the lives of fellow teenagers Louie, Willie, or Alfie. If the purpose of a unit on philosophy in literature is to ask students to think more deeply about life, death, and their place in the universe, then this succeeds: perfunctory discussions dissipate. Personal, passionate, probing exchanges vitalize literary discourse. Existential engagement in AP English . . . thanks to an unusual comparative approach.

From English Journal, *November 1989, 44–46*

2 Family Constellations: Teaching Dave Etter's "Brother"

Barbara Totherow

Brother

This is Halloween night, Andy.
The ghosts and goblins are going about,
costumed kids with their tricks and treats,
with their sacks full of candy and apples.
But I'm here, drinking from a pint of Antique,
the bourbon with the train on the label,
and gazing down at your moonlit headstone:

> Quentin Andrew Ficklin
> 1949 –1974

A cold wind is pouring stiff leaves
through the tall tree of heaven.
I smell frost and pine needles and weeds.
Oh, I feel sort of stupid coming to this place,
and, yes, a little phony, too.
Still, I do like these country graveyards.
They are always so full of crazy names
and sad angels with broken wings.
Listen, no one blames me for shooting you, boy.
Just an accident, they say.
It can happen, will happen, does happen.
Not that that changes things, of course.
Well, Andy, brothers we were, sure,
but never, ever friends, I guess.
And, if anything, being drunk and sentimental,
that's what devils me good tonight.
Hey, we sold your law books last week,
and we got a pretty fair price for them,
considering they were so beat up and all.
We hope the stamps and coins will go next.
You won't care, will you, Andy?
Boy, the other news isn't much.
Poor Bernice has got pimples real bad
and stays in her room day after day,
plunking, just plunking your blues guitar.
Dad is grouchy and is growing a beard.

Mom is silent as a slab of cheese.
But this, this is what you should know:
I aim to hunt only with loud strangers now.
Bang. Yell. Shout. Pheasants! Bang. Bang.
Brother, the Courthouse clock strikes ten.
I'm fixing to move away in your old boots.
They fit, boy. They're my new drinking boots.
The bottle's empty. All gone. Drunk up.
I'm going. I'm walking. I'm running.
Lord, Lord, the restless, relentless moon
stalks me through a death of black corn.*

—Dave Etter

Studying literature about family almost always seems to work, though I'm not sure why. Close to three-fourths of my high-school students come from anything but traditional families. They're in single-parent or second-family homes, and most of them seem to have such a complex of full-, half-, and step-siblings that even they wonder how they keep it all straight. It would seem an impossibility to find works that capture any kind of universal family experience, but, strangely, it's not. Maybe it's actually because of these very real complications of modern life that every time we read a story or poem about family conflict, everyone sits up. There's something inherently intriguing here. Maybe the kids from broken or second families are simply trying to find their own center of gravity. Maybe that's what kids even from traditional families need. Whatever it is, teenagers are willing to read, write, and talk about their own and literary families, even when other topics seem to leave them cold.

As part of a thematic unit on family, my "average-down" contemporary literature class focuses for a time on brother/sister relationships. There are three works about brothers I find especially fun to teach. One is a short story, "The Stone Boy" by Gina Berriault (1972), about a young boy who accidentally shoots his older brother. In shock, Arnold continues on to the garden to pick peas for an hour instead of racing home to confess the horror to his parents. As a result, he is ostracized by his family and neighbors for his apparent—and suspicious—lack of emotion.

The other two works are poems. Harley Elliot's "Brothers Together in Winter" shows an argument "about something one of us has or has not done" that flares into sudden violence as one boy takes a punch at his brother (1975, lines 7-9). The speaker's shocked final line, "and our faces are like mirrors" (27), reveals the stark intimacy only siblings can

---

*"Brother," by Dave Etter. Copyright © 1983. From *Alliance, Illinois*, Spoon River Poetry Press. Reprinted by permission of the author.

ever truly share. The third piece, Dave Etter's "Brother" (1976) continues this sharp focus on the themes of guilt and the love/hate complexity of almost any sibling relationship.

I love teaching Etter's poem. Right from the start, it's wonderful for often unmotivated kids with little self-confidence when it comes to reading poetry. To begin with, there's a clear, identifiable speaker. Since that's the first thing my students know they should look for, it's nice that this one is immediately obvious. It's even nicer that I don't have to convince them the author is not necessarily speaking for himself. Someone in class always catches the family name on the tombstone, and they clearly see that the writer does assume a separate persona.

Next, the intended listener of a poem is often ambiguous; maybe it's the reader, or maybe the speaker is talking to himself. The vagueness of the task can make identifying the listener frustrating, especially for the "mastery" learner who likes regularity and predictability. But even the least intuitive students know exactly who is talking to whom in this poem, and they can move on to the dramatic situation with confidence.

Setting is easy, too. The time is stated directly in line 1, and by line 7 we know the speaker is in the cemetery. Students easily find the clues that set the mood for this eerie, moonlit night of ghosts and goblins, and again, the mastery students, who rely on their senses for information, are told almost bluntly what the speaker sees, smells, feels, hears, and tastes. The details are concrete and plentiful, and I only have to sit back and listen as they move from setting to action, piecing together what is happening, what did happen, what's going to happen at the end.

This concreteness keeps them on track past the literal level and through the more difficult steps of analysis, and yet it's not just the less concrete, more intuitive thinkers who can handle all the possibilities of motivation: Why is the speaker here? Why is he drinking? Why is he moving away, and where is he going? They catch the significance of the action taking place on All Hallow's Eve, and they can talk about the ways we all are haunted by our own ghosts. But when I toss out the Freudian idea that there may be no such thing as an accident, most of them balk. "Of course it was an accident!"

So their next tasks send them to the text for close reading that involves both sensing and intuiting skills and requires them to use both logic and emotion: Find evidence to "prove" that the speaker may have felt real resentment toward his brother, that the accident was at least partly intended. Then on another sheet of paper, find evidence to prove the shooting was completely accidental and the speaker is truly grief-stricken. The "involvement" learners do this best with a partner or in small groups. I've had four work together in mini-debate teams, each pair looking for textual support to defend one thesis.

This close reading forces them to deal with subtleties of tone and tone change: When does the speaker sound flippant, nonchalant? At what points does he become suddenly intense? When does the bourbon seem to be slurring his voice? How can we tell? Though the students who rely on their feelings and intuitions to absorb information and reach conclusions have an easier time with this kind of thinking, there's still enough of the concrete here to keep the logical thinkers and those who depend on their senses involved. They can handle sleuthing like this within the poem, and they find convincing evidence for both sides.

Beyond the wonderfully ambiguous question of guilt, there are other intriguing questions. Again, the involvement thinkers, who learn best by relating everything to their own lives, are especially good at speculating about the family dynamics at work here: What are the roles and personalities of these family members? What were they before the accident? What might happen if this kind of tragedy happened to your own family? The creative thinkers, most able to see subtle connections, enjoy the drinking imagery. They see the irony of the "sad angels with broken wings" (line 17) and the implications of the Courthouse clock sounding the hour.

In context with the other two works we study, the poem takes on added richness. The speaker's regret that he and his brother were "never, ever friends" (23) echoes a passage in "The Stone Boy" when the sheriff asks young Arnold if he and his brother had been "good friends." Arnold is puzzled: "What did he mean—good friends? Eugie was his brother. That was different from a friend. . . . Eugie had had a way of looking at him, slyly and mockingly and yet confidentially, that had summed up how they both felt about being brothers. Arnold had wanted to be with Eugie more than with anybody else but he couldn't say they had been good friends" (61). This point of comparison is a good jumping off place for journal writing or discussion: To what extent are you and your brother or sister friends? In what ways are you the opposite of good friends? The writing allows them both to explore their own experience and get even closer to the experience of these two works.

In the same story, Arnold goes out on the day of his brother's funeral to take care of a job that "had been Eugie's" (66), and he seems startlingly older than the innocent nine-year-old he is in the beginning. In "Brother," the speaker takes over his dead brother's boots—fills his shoes, so to speak. "They fit, boy," he says cockily. "They're my new drinking boots" (line 42). This passage always seems to spark a good discussion that ties in with the guilt debate: Do brothers and sisters somehow want to take over their siblings' roles? Few students will admit to this, but most acknowledge envy of the freedom and autonomy that older brothers and sisters have, and many profess complete disgust with the "obvious" way their parents baby their younger siblings. At this point, I give them some psychological background.

Psychologists Rudolf Dreikurs and Loren Grey (1970) talk about the "family constellation" in which birth order, sex of the child, and the age differences between the children have an enormous effect on personality development. "Personality differences between siblings," they state, "are more often the result of their competitive striving than of heredity or other factors" (11). As they discuss the possible roles within this family constellation, Dreikurs and Grey note that "when the oldest child achieves competence in a certain area, the second child will rarely attempt to rival him in this area unless he feels he can overtake him or become better" (12). In this light, my students find it interesting that both Arnold in "The Stone Boy" and the speaker of "Brother" move into their brothers' territories only after these latter two are dead. Andy's brother even tells him casually, "Hey, we sold your law books last week, / . . . / We hope the stamps and coins will go next" (26, 29). Is there secret satisfaction that all the belongings, perhaps even the brother's memory, are being eliminated?

Even more dramatically interesting to the students are psychologist Haim Ginott's comments on brother/sister conflict. I usually read them parts of the chapter on "Jealousy" from Ginott's *Between Parent and Child* (1965), in which he flatly states that even if it is not overtly apparent, sibling rivalry is a part of every family. "Jealousy, envy, and rivalry," he says, "will inevitably be there" (146). This envy originates, he claims, in "an infant's desire to be his mother's only 'dearly beloved.' This desire is so possessive that it tolerates no rivals. When brothers and sisters arrive, the child competes with them for the *exclusive* love of both parents" (152).

These psychological theories suggest some interesting answers to explain why family literature is so intriguing to children in nontraditional, second families, with their own complex "constellations" of full-, half-, and step-siblings. But these theories also offer all kinds of interesting questions as we discuss our three works on brothers: Have Eugie's and Andy's deaths allowed their brothers to shed inferior self-images and assume a higher status in their families, if only in their own eyes? If a young man can take over his brother's boots, has he then managed to eliminate this rival for his parents' exclusive love?

Harley Elliot's poem, "Brothers Together in Winter," emphasizes this overt rivalry far more than either of the other two works and seems to give credence to Ginott's theories, especially when the speaker says matter-of-factly, "Yes, we are going/ to kill each other this time/ once and for all" (lines 5–7). But the speaker's shocked final line, as his brother's clenched fist shears by his chin, "and our faces are like mirrors" (27), adds a new dimension: Do we just see our own jealousy and anger reflected in the face of a brother or sister, or is a sibling the closest thing we have to self? Do Arnold in "The Stone Boy" and the speaker in "Brother" agonize just over their brothers' deaths and their own guilt, or has each lost a part of himself, as well?

Students who are supposedly "average-down" can handle this kind of philosophical thinking, and they bring surprising honesty and sophistication to the discussion. Again, the complexities of modern family life perhaps give today's teenagers a much more experienced view of family relationships than those of us from simpler, more traditional family backgrounds can ever know.

In conjunction with Berriault's story and Elliot's poem, "Brother" becomes a complex, multi-leveled study. Even without the parallels and connections with these other works, however, the reading experience of a poem like "Brother" is a rich one for high-school students. It creates its own echoes, like the ripples expanding outward when a stone is dropped into a pond. Readers, especially teenagers, remember it long after they leave it.

Maybe what I like best about teaching this poem, though, is that it's always successful. My often uninterested students like the poem and are willing to work with it. There's drama here, and there's depth that is accessible. The kinds of questions I'm trying to teach them to bring to any poem are the ones that get clear answers here. It's a confidence-booster, the kind of poem that makes them willing to try reading poetry again—even on their own.

Works Cited

Berriault, Gina. 1972. "The Stone Boy." *The Family*. Ed. Hannah Beate Haupt, Lilla Heston, Joy Littell, and Sarah Solotaroff. Evanston: McDougal, 55–67.

Dreikurs, Rudolf, and Loren Grey. 1970. *A Parent's Guide to Child Discipline*. New York: Hawthorn.

Elliot, Harley. 1975. "Brothers Together in Winter." *In Touch*. New York: Harcourt, 79.

Etter, Dave. 1976. "Brother." *Literature Lives!* (Blue Level). Ed. Hannah Beate
   Haupt, Lilla Heston, Joy Littell, and Sarah Solotaroff. Evanston: McDou-
   gal, 496–97.
Ginott, Haim G. 1965. *Between Parent and Child.* New York: Avon, 145–57.

From English Journal, *November 1988, 78–81*

3 Teaching Critical Analysis Writing Using Stephen King's *Danse Macabre*

Michael Begg

Too often, I'm questioned by my eleventh grade honors composition students about the purpose of learning various writing techniques. Sure, they understand and master the use of definition, comparison/contrast, cause/effect, etc., in a simple five-paragraph essay. But outside of the classroom setting, they find little use for writing. And it's important to encourage students to extend themselves beyond the simple structure or format that composition teachers stress. A critical analysis paper can be a worthwhile assignment that can offer students the opportunities to apply writing to their everyday interests.

What seems to interest most teenagers is fashion, music, television and movies, and sports. It is sometimes hard for them to judge the quality involved in some of these areas. As a result, some fall into the fads and trends of fashion and music, look up to only those sports figures who have been widely publicized, and watch television shows and movies that appeal to them at a level that fails to challenge them intellectually. As teachers, especially composition teachers, it's important for us to develop students' critical skills, and writing is an excellent means for analysis.

In searching for a topic area of high interest for my students to write about critically, I ran across Stephen King's *Danse Macabre*. Mistakenly placed on many bookstores' shelves with the author's works of fiction, it is an excellent model of critical analysis writing. King explores the horror genre (movies, television, fiction) and attempts to explain why audiences find it so appealing. He analyzes many films, always with a critical eye. What encouraged me to choose this book for my classes to read, besides the obvious attraction teenagers have for horror, was a short passage in the second chapter:

> I've tried here to delineate some of the differences between science fiction and horror, science fiction and fantasy, terror and horror, horror and revulsion, more by example than by definition. All of which is very well, but perhaps we ought to examine the emotion of

> horror a little more closely—not in terms of definition but in terms
> of effect. What does horror do? Why do people want to be horrified
> . . . why do they pay to be horrified? Why an *Exorcist*? A *Jaws*?
> An *Alien*?
>   But before we talk about why people crave the effect, maybe we
> ought to spend a little time thinking about components—and if we
> do not choose to define horror itself, we can at least examine the
> elements and perhaps draw some conclusions from them.

Perhaps without realizing it, King has explained to the reader his
intention to analyze by using the simple writing techniques of
comparison/contrast, example, definition, and cause/effect. With this
in mind, *Danse Macabre* became the primary source of the critical
analysis paper assignment—a culmination of all the techniques and
strategies that the composition students have learned.

To begin, students made use of videotapes of the major films King
discusses in his book. Each student was assigned to watch three films
similar in theme. No more than three students were assigned to the same
group of films. The films and the writing topics varied. From the dozens
of areas that King explores, the topics included some like

> *The Abominable Dr. Phibes, The Tomb of Ligeia,* and *The Body
> Snatcher:* The horror films that derive their best effects from the fear
> of dying.
>
> *The Hunchback of Notre Dame* (1939), *Werewolf of London* (1935),
> the *Elephant Man:* The horror film as an invitation to indulge in
> deviant anti-social behavior by proxy.
>
> *The Thing from Another World* (1951), *The Day the Earth Stood
> Still,* and *Invasion of the Body Snatchers:* Science fiction films
> reflecting political fears rather than supernatural fears.
>
> *The Fly* (1958), *The Omega Man, Dr. Cyclops:* Horror films with a
> technological subtext—those films that suggest that we have been
> betrayed by our own machines and processes of mass production.
>
> *The Fly* (1958), *Cat People* (1942), and *The Man with the X-Ray
> Eyes:* The modern American horror film and how it exploits the
> real fears of normal people.
>
> *Plan 9 from Outer Space, Attack of the 50 Ft. Woman,* and *The
> Little Shop of Horrors:* The horror movie as junk food—why have
> there been so many bad horror films?
>
> *The Ghostbreakers* (1940), *The Haunting,* and *The Changeling:*
> The primal haunted house story—how its subtext addresses our
> more concrete fears, whether they be social, economic, cultural, or
> political.
>
> *The Mummy* (1932), *The Mummy* (1959) and *The Picture of
> Dorian Gray:* Horror films depicting the mythic fairy tale of man's
> quest for immortality and its inevitable fight with humanity.

Frankenstein (1931), *The Bride of Frankenstein,* and *The Curse of Frankenstein* (1957): Exploring the Frankenstein myth—humanity as an insufficient god.

Psycho, The Birds, Frenzy: Alfred Hitchcock—master of suspense. Putting the audience's world in chaos.

The Raven (1935), *The Black Cat* (1934), and *The Body Snatcher:* Horrific Imaginings: Boris Karloff and Bela Lugosi—masters of Macabre.

Dracula (1931), *The Wolfman,* and *Frankenstein* (1931): The monsters representing our lusher concepts of evil in the modern horror story—the vampire, the werewolf, and the thing without a name.

Once the films had been seen, there were a series of guidelines for the students to follow in critically analyzing their three films. They included:

1. The writer must base his or her analysis on the ideas discussed in *Danse Macabre.*
2. Research is required. A minimum of three sources from the library is necessary. (School librarians compiled a reserve list for this assignment.)
3. The writer must consciously make use of the variety of writing techniques we have studied, just as Stephen King does in *Danse Macabre.* Definition, comparison/contrast, process, cause/effect, classification, and argumentation can all be used effectively. Even the narrative technique can be put to good use; King uses it in his chapter entitled "An Annoying Autobiographical Pause."
4. Within the paper the writer must briefly provide a synopsis of the plot of each film. *Briefly* is the key word; the paper is not a simple retelling of their stories.
5. The writer must make use of specific scenes and/or lines of dialog from the films to illustrate and support ideas. When referring to a particular aspect of the film, the person responsible should be attributed. For example, all aspects involving the visual storytelling would be attributed to the director. Matters concerning the actual story events/plots would be attributed to the screenwriter, etc. It is important to refer to the production credits and cast that is included in a variety of the books on the library's reserve list.
6. After analyzing specific aspects that the topic demands, the writer must present a final judgment, a criticism of each film. Does it succeed within the horror genre?
7. Before turning in the actual paper, each group will make an oral presentation to the class. The presentations will reflect all of the information gathered within the above guidelines. (I've suggest-

ed to my students to watch *Siskel and Ebert At the Movies* to get
an idea of how to make their presentations.)

8. The paper to be turned in would include a title page, an outline
   page, a formal copy of the body of the paper, a footnote page, and
   a bibliography.

In the presentations and papers, it was obvious that students had
begun to sharpen their critical skills. Many felt that they would not have
appreciated these *old* films if they had not examined their subtexts. The
students came away from the viewings with more weighing on their
minds than just the simple entertainment value of each film. For
example, one whose topic dealt with Boris Karloff and Bela Lugosi in
The Raven, The Black Cat, and *The Body Snatcher* observed how the
presentation of the speech patterns and dialog of the two stars suggested
genuinely frightening connotations. One who wrote on *The Fly, The
Omega Man,* and *Dr. Cyclops* concluded that "techno-horror" films
effectively create fear when they show that it is not humans or machines
which bring about tragedy—but the combination of the two. And
finally, a student commenting on *The Hunchback of Notre Dame* noted
that it is an atypical horror film.

> It is one that is unusual because we watch as the characters
> experience terror, but we experience little of it ourselves. In this
> manner, the fears that we share in common with the characters are
> released, making us feel better.

From the discussions generated by the presentations, it became clear
to everyone that horror films do not necessarily need special effects,
gross makeup, or buckets of blood. Many agreed that the trends in recent
horror films (such as *Friday the 13th* and other "slasher movies" and
Alien and "gross-out movies" like it) portray evil as something external.
They felt that they were not as effective as those films which suggest that
evil rests in humanity. Why else, some concluded, would Hollywood
choose to remake horror classics like *Invasion of the Body Snatchers,
The Thing, Invaders From Mars, Cat People, It! The Terror From
Beyond Space* (remade as *Alien*), and *The Fly?* They can also see that the
remakes often fail in creating horror by attempting to update the stories
with special effects.

As a result of their intensive writing assignment, students became
aware of how to apply writing techniques to their own interests. Soon
after, many attempted to analyze albums of rock groups; some wanted to
do an analysis of clothing styles; others even attempted to critically
overview the teams participating in the summer's upcoming Goodwill

Games. In any case, all were sure not to make their judgments until they had performed a satisfactory analysis.

Bibliography

Here is a partial list of some of the best reference books on horror films:

Cohen, Daniel. *Horror in the Movies*. New York: Clarion, 1982.

Cohen, Daniel. *Horror Movies*. New York: Gallery Books, 1984.

Everson, William. *Classics of the Horror Film*. Secaucus, New Jersey: Citadel, 1974.

Frank, Alan. *The Horror Film Handbook*. New York: Barnes and Noble, 1982.

King, Stephen. *Danse Macabre*. New York: Berkley, 1981.

Moore, Darrell. *The Best, Worst, and Most Unusual Horror Films*. Skokie, Illinois: Publications International Limited, 1983.

Schoell, William. *Stay Out of the Shower*. New York: Dember Books, 1985.

Strick, Philip. *Science Fiction Movies*. London: Octopus Books, 1976.

Weldon, Michael. *The Psychotronic Encyclopedia of Film*. New York: Ballantine, 1983.

From English Journal, *March 1987, 72-74*

4 Gypsies, Jews, and
The Merchant of Venice

Thomas McKendy

For many years *The Merchant of Venice* was as much a part of high-school education in North America as algebra, football, or the teaching of grammar. Recently, however, many teachers, parents, and others have had serious second thoughts about the play. They worry that Shakespeare's distorted presentation of Jews may create or reinforce stereotypes in immature minds and that these stereotypes may seem to be endorsed by the reputation of Shakespeare or the authority of the school and teacher. In 1986, for example, a series of incidents involving name-calling, anti-Semitic graffiti, and the throwing of coins at Jewish students led the Waterloo, Ontario, school board to withdraw the play from the ninth-grade curriculum. Writing in the Toronto *Globe and Mail*, Gunther Plaut (July 22, 1986, A7) and Michele Landsberg (July 26, 1986, A2) have argued convincingly that, granted the wealth of literature available for teaching, *The Merchant of Venice* should not be taught before grade eleven or twelve.

Even teachers of older students, however, need to think carefully about how to present the play. Although such students are presumably impervious to simple stereotypes, they often have much to learn about prejudice. A careful look at Shakespeare's prejudices and their roots can teach students not only about historical attitudes but about their own unacknowledged assumptions as well.

Many college students have already studied *The Merchant of Venice* in high school. Unfortunately, my students report that the issue of anti-Semitism in the play has been generally overshadowed in the classroom by questions of plot, character, irony, and the like. When the issue is raised at all, discussion usually focuses on Shylock's defense of his humanity: "Hath not a Jew eyes? . . . If you prick us do we not bleed?" (III.i). As proof that Shakespeare was, in fact, a warm human being who repudiated the cruel behavior of his characters, this speech is usually considered sufficient—or, occasionally, insufficient. Such treatment neither acknowledges the seriousness of Shakespeare's distortions nor adequately explains how an otherwise humane and compassionate man could create such an odious misrepresentation. In general, students who have thought about the issue at all consider Shakespeare either a simple bigot or a kind of harmless antique, a quaint portrayer of attitudes no longer taken very seriously.

Of course, neither of these views deals with the actual complexities of history or of modern prejudice. One way of highlighting these complexities before students begin reading the play is to look at their own culture's attitudes towards gypsies.

Gypsies have a number of important similarities to Elizabethan Jews. Traditionally, they have no homeland, living as outsiders in most societies of the western world. Like the Jews, they were singled out for extermination by the Nazis, and hence prejudice against gypsies has been a source of immense suffering in the twentieth century—a fact virtually unknown among non-Jewish students. Moreover, Jews and Gentiles alike are likely to hold a fairly complex set of stereotypes about gypsies that have not been modified by discussion and consciousness-raising as some of their other prejudices may have been. For example, most of them use the verb "to gyp" (probably a derivative of "gypsy" according to the *O.E.D.* and *Webster's Third*) as synonym for "to cheat," although most would be shocked by similar use of the verb "to jew," a usage that is still common enough to be included in most unabridged dictionaries. Finally, the students' stereotypes of gypsies are usually not so strong or so emotionally rooted in their own experiences and fears as to inhibit self-examination.

In any case, before beginning to study *The Merchant of Venice*, students can be asked to jot down in five or ten minutes everything they know or have heard about gypsies.

Predictably, their "knowledge" includes a number of common stereotypes. In my students' eyes, gypsies are hot-tempered and carefree; they have large families and travel from place to place in caravans, cheating the unwary and stealing their children; gypsies wear loose-fitting clothes with lots of bracelets and earrings; they play the violin and read fortunes from crystal balls or cards; there is always a king.

Now few of my students are naive enough to believe that this set of descriptions presents an accurate view of what actual gypsies are like, although there are occasional claims of factual accuracy: "They sometimes steal babies. (That's true. It happened to my great-grandmother in Romania. I'm not joking!)" Most of the students acknowledge that their views are stereotypes, drawn largely from children's books, popular movies, and television commercials. Only a few are aware of ever having seen a gypsy, and virtually none have ever talked to gypsies. They do not know what language gypsies speak, what religion they practice, or what foods they eat.

The fact is, however, that stereotypes do not simply evaporate once they are identified. The images in our heads may affect our behavior and our attitudes even when we recognize that those images are inaccurate. I ask my students to imagine themselves or their friends writing a story or a television script in which one of the characters is a gypsy. It is possible, I suppose, that the gypsy character will be a neurosurgeon, a police chief, or an English teacher. But I doubt it. Similarly, if the script included a fortune teller, I suspect that that character would more likely be a gypsy than a German, an Australian, or a Japanese.

The point of all this, of course, is that my students' views of gypsies resemble in many ways the kinds of views Shakespeare probably had about Jews. He had most likely never seen nor spoken with a Jew. The few Jews living in England in his day probably were converts to Christianity and, therefore, like Jessica in the play, not "really" Jews. He would have known that Jews on the continent were often money-lenders, a profession closed to Christians because of religious laws against lending money at interest, and that these moneylenders were despised as usurers. Jews for Shakespeare, like gypsies for my students, were a somewhat exotic and largely unknown people. They were perhaps an abstraction to him, and as such he was probably no more hostile to them than my students are to gypsies.

None of this, however, precluded Shakespeare from including an offensive and degrading picture of a Jew when he needed a two-dimensional villain for his play. In fact, Shylock's Jewishness was particularly appropriate to Shakespeare's purposes because it served as a sort of shorthand for a cluster of notions about mercy and justice derived from the way Elizabethans interpreted the Bible. To the Elizabethans, a Jew was a sort of imperfect Christian who had embraced only half of God's message, the Old Testament. The Old Testament, in turn, represented the covenant of justice, law, and vengeance rather than the new covenant of mercy, forgiveness, and love suggested by the Sermon on the Mount.

This Elizabethan perception of the Jews of the Old Testament sets up the major theme of *The Merchant of Venice*, the opposition of mercy and justice, as personified in the characters of Portia and Shylock. That Shylock is legalistic and unforgiving is not central to the moral vision of the play; certainly no attempt is made to focus on his repentance or reform after the trial. That Antonio, Bassanio, and Gratiano are equally legalistic and unforgiving, however, is absolutely central. They ought to embody Christian values, but in fact they seem no more virtuous than young men usually are. Even Antonio, often praised for his friendship and generosity, in fact lends money only to his friends. Do not even tax collectors do the same?

Specifically, the Christian men in *The Merchant of Venice* do not embody Christian mercy and forgiveness, as Shylock well knows: "And if you wrong us, shall we not revenge? If we are like you in the rest, we will resemble you in that. . . . The villainy you teach me, I will execute" (III, i). At the trial, they accept Shylock's terms of reference, and when the law is on their side, they enforce the law. The Duke offers pardon but threatens to recant it unless Shylock accepts Antonio's conditions. Bassanio and Gratiano do not at all understand Portia's message about the quality of mercy until they, too, find themselves in need of love and forgiveness for their broken vows about the rings in Act V.

By making Shylock a Jew, Shakespeare is able to develop this theme efficiently and powerfully for his Elizabethan Christian audience in a way he could not do if Shylock belonged to some other despised group, perhaps the Irish or even the gypsies. Shakespeare does not have to develop Shylock's character in much detail, because he is able to use the stereotype of the vengeful Jew. Because the tension between law, justice, and revenge on the one hand and love, mercy, and forgiveness on the other is a central, if more subtle, theme in much of Shakespeare's mature work (*Measure for Measure, King Lear, The Tempest, The Winter's Tale*), this play is a particularly useful introduction to Shakespeare.

In teaching *The Merchant of Venice,* we must make clear that Shakespeare seems to have shared the prejudices of his time and culture, apparently without the reflection or self-examination that we would expect from any sensitive person in our time and culture. If our students realize that they, too, may harbor such unexamined biases, about gypsies for example, that realization may lead them to a greater understanding of the weaknesses of others—Shakespeare would have approved—and to a more sensitive awareness of their own shortcomings, even when not conscious or malicious.

Nevertheless, students must not be left to think that such biases and stereotypes, conscious or not, are trivial or tolerable (though they may be forgivable). In our own century, such casual stereotypes have almost certainly smoothed the way for more vicious prejudices, for the persecution and slaughter of Jews, gypsies, and others. Shakespeare was not a twentieth-century anti-Semite in period costume, but those of us who teach his plays must take responsibility for seeing that his message of mercy is neither misinterpreted as a rationale for anti-Semitism nor hidden from view by our guilt for our own quite different sins.

From English Journal, *November 1988, 24–26*

5 Hidings and Revelations: Robert Hayden's "The Whipping"

Linda Wyman

The Whipping

The old woman across the way
  is whipping the boy again
and shouting to the neighborhood
  her goodness and his wrongs.

Wildly he crashes through elephant ears,
  pleads in dusty zinnias,
while she in spite of crippling fat
  pursues and corners him.

She strikes and strikes the shrilly circling
  boy till the stick breaks
in her hand. His tears are rainy weather
  to woundlike memories:

My head gripped in bony vise
  of knees, the writhing struggle
to wrench free, the blows, the fear
  worse than blows that hateful

Words would bring, the face that I
  no longer knew or loved . . .
Well, it is over now, it is over,
  and the boy sobs in his room,

And the woman leans muttering against
  a tree, exhausted, purged—
avenged in part for lifelong hidings
  she has had to bear.*

—Robert Hayden

"This is a poem about reality," someone almost always says, and no one with whom I've ever read Robert Hayden's "The Whipping" has ever said otherwise.

---

*"The Whipping" is reprinted from *Collected Poems* of Robert Hayden, Edited by Frederick Glaysher, by permission of Liveright Publishing Corporation. Copyright © 1985 by Erma Hayden.

Students' immediate identification and sympathy are with the boy who is getting the whipping. There are often some nervous, survivor-proud laughs at "again," and I have only to ask what kinds of things a person giving a whipping ever says about "her goodness and his wrongs" to discover that everyone in the room can answer:

> I cook, I clean . . . and you act like a heathen.
>
> After all I've done for you, look how you behave. . . .
>
> I've tried to teach you right from wrong. . . .
>
> I've worked my fingers to the bone for you. . . .
>
> I'm only doing this for your own good. . . .
>
> I'm whipping you because I love you.

We are clearly in familiar territory.

The language of "The Whipping" is as accessible as the experience depicted in its first stanzas. If the poem is read in a group, there is no need for a dictionary. When I read it recently with two classes of students in remedial English and with several small groups of advanced students, there was always someone who knew the meaning of whatever word was unfamiliar to another. "What's a vise?" "You know, that thing in a woodworking shop." The questioner, watching the respondent's miming hands, nods: "Oh. That thing you turn." What are zinnias? Oh—those bright flowers that grow all summer. Elephant ears? Oh: *that's* what those big leaves are called. *Purged?* "You know [with laughter], like when you need a big dose." The ugliness and terror of lines five through ten communicate themselves unerringly: almost everyone can identify *wildly, crashes, pleads, corners,* and *shrilly* as words which express panic, and students nod their understanding when Brian remarks that "the mobility of the extraordinarily fat woman" is in itself terrifying.

Typically, students have no problems in reading the poem until line eleven: "His tears are rainy weather/to woundlike memories." Those who have difficulty have not been aware, until this point, of the poem's third character, the speaker/onlooker. ("I thought that was just the poet talking," someone explains.) A question about the implications of "across the way," in line one, is usually enough to establish the presence of the person watching the whipping. Students offer questions to help classmates for whom this line is still unclear. "How does rainy weather make *you* feel?" they ask. "What kind of mood does it put *you* in?" Well then, they reason, if "his tears" make "rainy weather," it is not surprising that an outpouring of "woundlike memories" should follow. That the memories are those of the speaker/onlooker is confirmed, of course, by *My* at the beginning of stanza four. ("There's only one person in this poem who could say 'My.'")

The "woundlike memories" evoke murmurs of recollection. If the readers have not actually had their heads "gripped in bony vise of knees" (and one tells that he has), they all remember— or feel that they remember—the writhing, the blows, the hateful words, the fearsomely changed faces. The ellipsis and the resumption of present tense make clear that the speaker's memories have receded. Someone asks, "Why does he say twice that 'it is over'?" I reply, "How many things are over?"

When both the dreadful whipping and the painful memories are "over," the language of the poem eases off, the *and-* joined clauses suggesting the restoration of an order, however grim. Cheryll and Rusty point out that the poem's frenzied movement stops when the old woman is "purged," and we, like her, are ready to "lean against a tree." *Exhausted,* in the last stanza, applies as well to persons reading the poem as to those who are in it. If I ask about the meaning of *hidings,* however, we discover that our most intense discussion is yet to come.

Usually, students say that *hidings* refers to those experiences in the woman's life which she has kept secret, and certainly there is no denying the word's associations with *to hide.* When I ask, however, if "hidings" are what my students call things that they have hidden or kept secret, no one ever says that this is the case. "How have you heard the word?" I ask. "Have you ever heard anything called 'a hiding'?" Often there is someone who has heard it: I'll tan your hide for that. I'll give you a hiding you won't forget. The discovery that a hiding is a whipping brings a surge of response. The recursiveness of child abuse is, after all, a phenomenon to which our attention has often been called in recent years. Students often are ready to believe that "the old woman" whips the boy because she has been beaten as a child—until someone notices *lifelong:* "for lifelong hidings she has had to bear." Once students take in the implications of "lifelong," they begin to comprehend Hayden's stunning, poem-unifying metaphor. The old woman has "taken a beating" all her life. This poem has three victims—not one, as we'd supposed in the opening stanza, or two as we'd learned in the third.

Realizing that the cycle of pain is much larger than we had thought sends us back through the poem again and leads us to discover that we know much more than we believed we had known. We wonder what kinds of beatings the old woman has taken. Quite possibly she *was* whipped as a child, we agree. Ann points out that for an elderly, terribly fat person to have charge of a young boy could in itself be a punishing experience. ("*Yes,* he's young! An older kid wouldn't be so hysterical— and, besides, he could get away!") Someone notices *dusty* in line six and suggests that the old woman is having to fight to have any flowers at all—her yard, at any rate, is a far cry from that field of purple flowers in *The Color Purple*. That zinnias and elephant ears will grow under less than optimal gardening conditions points both to the old woman's determination to have something besides pain in her life and to the odds against her doing so. Rusty and Ann relate the woman's being avenged "in part" to her whipping the boy "again"; she is never completely avenged. Corey observes that both the speaker and the old woman have "internal scars"; the memories, after all, are wound-*like*. The boy is hearing "hateful words" such as the speaker remembers. Matthew realizes that whereas the woman's way to deal with her hidings has been to whip the boy, the speaker's way may well have been to write the poem.

Is this poem about child abuse? I ask. My students are adamant: No. Though Cheryll has called our attention repeatedly to the fierce energy in the poem, and though most of us have cringed at the image of the woman's striking and striking until the stick breaks, no one believes that the whipping has occurred "for no reason at all" or that the boy's wounds will require medical attention. For most of the students with whom I read the poem, child abuse entails a certain hideous wantonness: "You know," one of them says, "you be in the bed and your mother come home and beat up on you." None of us minimizes the savagery of the boy's whipping, but by extending our sympathies to the onlooker and finally to the old woman, Hayden has made it impossible for us to feel that any hot-line that we might call could provide the relief that is needed here.

"This poem is about how people really feel," Joyce says. Louvenia adds passionately, "My mama—that lady loves me to death, but she whips me. Things *are* awful." Things are awful, and reading Robert Hayden's "The Whipping" lets us glimpse why that is so.

From English Journal, *March 1988, 82–84*

6 Imaginary Gardens, Real Toads: Wallace's "Ungainly Things"

Elizabeth D. Nelms and Ben F. Nelms

Ungainly Things

A regular country toad—pebbly,
   squat,
      shadow-green

as the shade of the spruces
   in the garden
      he came from—rode

to Paris in a hatbox
   to Lautrec's
      studio (skylights

on the skies of Paris);
   ate
      cutworms from a box,

hopped
   occasionally
      among the furniture and easels,

while the clumsy little painter
   studied
      him in charcoal

until he was beautiful.
   One day
      he found his way

down stairs toward the world
   again,
      into the streets of Montmartre,

and, missing him, the painter-dwarf
   followed,
      peering among cobbles

laughed at, searching
   until long past dark
      the length of the Avenue Frochot,

over and over,
for the fisted, marble-eyed
fellow
no one would ever see again
except
in sketches that make ungainly things beautiful.*

—Robert Wallace

Students still come to us with a number of misconceptions about poetry. They think it is about pretty things—flowers, trees, sunsets, love, God, and nature. We like to share poems with them that show poets finding their subjects among ordinary and mundane realities. Like Marianne Moore, we like to think of poems as "imaginary gardens with real toads in them." Students think poetry should sound a certain way—rhyme, alliteration, and a thumping good rhythm, ta-dum, ta-dum, ta-dum. We like to share poems in which the sound effects are subtler, which counterpoint line to syntax. But, most important, students think poems are difficult, fraught with unfamiliar words, curious sentence inversions, and "hidden" meanings. We like to share poems that are fairly direct, which require at the most an ordinary dictionary and/or desk encyclopedia to decipher meaning. We like to show them poems that allow them to work out meaning for themselves; that don't require them to rely on us. Such a poem is Robert Wallace's "Ungainly Things." Its title, its subject, and its theme all celebrate the potential glory of misshapen, common, unlovely realities. We present this poem to high-school students so that they make that discovery for themselves. (Except where indicated, all the quoted comments come from sophomores in a regular track—not honors!) On first reading, the poem could make them fly for cover. What? No rhyme? A poem about an ugly old toad? What's with these crazy lines? They don't match. Since the poem may jar their sensibilities, we prepare them for the content as the poet probably expected his readers to be prepared. We write the name "Toulouse" on the board and ask if anyone associates another name with it. If no one responds, we scrawl "Lautrec" up beside the first name. The class begins to brainstorm, with the teacher writing down every association, both wild and on-target: *artist, French, ugly, deformed, alcoholic, drugs, sex, Moulin Rouge, dancing girls, hollow cane, dead, Paris, depressed, famous, "too loose."* After about five minutes—sometimes a probing question helps generate a bit more ("Artist—of what?")—the board is filled. But to move toward clarity, we have students get in small groups and note five specific questions they

---

*"Ungainly Things" from *Ungainly Things,* © 1968 by Robert Wallace.

would like answered about Toulouse-Lautrec. They list ones like the following: Who was this man? Why was he famous? When did he live? What exactly did he paint? Was he sexually involved? How ugly was he?

At this point, students are given access to a cart which we have filled with simple reference books from the library. Each group chooses a dictionary, encyclopedia, or art reference book and, for the next seven minutes, tries to find answers to as many questions as they can. They also jot down any other interesting information they find; they find out a lot in just seven minutes. Passages are read which describe the artist-dwarf, misshapen by an accident in youth. Misinformation is cleared up, and they begin to feel well-informed and interested. (We don't know whether Toulouse-Lautrec is in E. D. Hirsch's book of essential knowledge or not, but we do know that seven minutes with readily available reference books can provide the kind of background information that literate persons bring to their reading. That's the point of this exercise. You don't have to know everything to read knowledgeably; you can "look it up.")

This introduction takes about twenty-five minutes, and the pace has been lively. Finally, a few prints of Lautrec's posters are displayed. Now students are ready for the reading of the poem. After a quick check to see that they have a sense of the meaning of *ungainly*, we read the poem aloud twice. The poem is projected on an overhead, or students are given copies as we read. Then they write for ten minutes, exploring their immediate responses to the poem, some hesitating, making false-starts, but most rapidly filling a page. Because we have only fifty minutes, the period ends at this point.

The next class period begins with the sharing of papers or ideas which surfaced in the ten-minute writings. No teacher is needed to decipher the "meaning" of the poem, for students teach one another, reinforcing initial impressions, extending understanding, challenging vague or off-base notions. They read passages from their free writings:

> Whenever I read a poem, I always think the author is trying to tell me something using something else.
>
> —Amy

> An artist is able to catch people's eyes to make them look at a simple little toad, an animal which no one pays much attention to.

> An artist helps open people's eyes so they can see Toulouse-Lautrec once painted his bedroom. Nothing was really special about it. It had a bed, a chair, and a desk and some pictures on the wall. I still liked the painting though, because it was colorful and well done. If

I painted my bedroom, it would be boring and would not hold anyone's interest. But his room did.

—Shannon

Of course, not all students "tune in" to any one poem, but of the more than 150 to whom we have presented this poem this year, only eleven have expressed indifference or distaste. Many of them relate to Lautrec on the basis of their own experiences:

I think this poet was also talking about the feeling we all get sometimes of being bizarre. The poem changes your mood depending on how it is read. If you read it with a soft voice, you can almost feel the hurt of being lost and laughed at. If you read it in just a regular voice with an I-don't-care attitude, it's really a cruel poem. No one likes to be laughed at.

—Stacey

I know the artist was laughed at because I'm not even half that ugly and I get made fun of all the time.

—Unsigned sophomore paper

I empathize with this gentle, caring man through Robert Wallace's poem. I feel somewhat guilty for the taunting he must have endured although I am not responsible for it. To think that this artist had only his lithographs to speak to the outside world for him.

—Lon, senior

Jocelyn writes, "It's interesting to see how people show their artistic ability through the strangest things." The poet himself made that very point in an introduction to the poem. "A good subject," he says, "stumbled on at the right moment, becomes a way of expressing our ideas and feelings. It can release, shape, focus them, as we might not be able to do directly. Often enough, it will even reveal ideas and feelings we weren't aware of having" (Wallace 146).

A new admiration for the artist and poet is kindled as the students feel the impact of the message.

The artist saw things differently than many other people, but he did all he could to make others see the beauty in all things, even ungainly things. I admire people who can do that.

—Tracy

As we read this next paper, we are reminded of Coleridge's haunted mariner, who roamed the earth, searching for someone who would listen to his message:

When I read about the people laughing and staring at him like he
had "lost it," I realize that this is the way a lot of people react when
they don't understand or agree with what they see, hear, or read.

—Amy

These students, who shouted wild guesses across the room just the day
before, have a new awareness of the artist. Just as Toulouse-Lautrec
immortalized the toad, Robert Wallace helped them feel that they knew
the artist.

There is a trace of cruelty in this poem when the poet talks of
Toulouse-Lautrec being laughed at and ridiculed by others. This
makes me feel sorry for this unique little man.

To me this poem is sad and really makes me understand about
Toulouse-Lautrec's life. If I'd never done any reading on this man
and read this poem, I think I'd know a lot about him. I feel as if I
know him without knowing him.

—Angi

We agree with this student that the poem may not need our careful
groundwork, but other students voice this comment: "If we hadn't
talked about the artist before this poem, it would have made no sense
at all."

What we provide as teachers is a trusting atmosphere and an open
forum in which ideas can flourish and questions can be asked, a gift of
time and a bit of information, and an impetus encouraging students to
work at deciphering the code themselves. As their understanding
deepens, one sees an almost cocky look which says in so many words,
"Hey, we get it and no one had to tell us the answer."

I think this poem is making some kind of comparison to a toad and
Toulouse-Lautrec in that they both are ugly to ordinary eyes but art
makes them beautiful.

—Wendy

I think this poem was written in metaphor with the toad actually
representing Toulouse-Lautrec, who was also ungainly, yet his
work on canvas was beautiful like the toad in charcoal. So,
although he didn't paint himself beautifully, his paintings show
the beauty in other things, which reflect back onto this crippled
painter.

—Eric

The French artist is made beautiful in this poem. They are rather an
ungainly pair, Toulouse-Lautrec and that toad.

—David, senior

As teachers, we confirm their emerging insights by contributing this account by the poet of how he stumbled upon his subject in the following story about Toulouse-Lautrec.

> A friend sent him in a hat box, from L'Isle Adam, a large toad which hopped about his apartment for days, becoming quite a pet. At last it escaped into the "wilderness" of the rue Caulaincourt (Montmartre quarter, in Paris). Toulouse-Lautrec, a far more affectionate and soft-hearted man than some biographers have represented him, was desolate. When the rumour came later that the toad had been seen on the Avenue Frochot, he spent hours searching for him—the length of that street! (Lautrec, *A Bestiary,* in Wallace 148)

The poet goes on to comment: "I retold the story. It was a way of expressing my feeling about the beauty in the ordinary, which we all too easily accept as dull and boring, and about the role of art in helping us to recapture simple wonder. But in writing the poem I discovered something I didn't know I was thinking, about the role of the artist. There is only one toad in the poem, but the title is plural" (Wallace 146). Of course, the students have already picked up on all these "meanings," but they enjoy hearing how the poet "discovered" what he meant. We conclude our discussion by posting on the bulletin board two sketches by Lautrec, juxtaposed: a self-portrait caricature and the squatty toad.

Students have found several real toads in this imaginary garden, and have come to appreciate them. We hope that, no matter what we do to present poet/artists to our students, we will do so in a way that the poet/artist will not be rejected but welcomed as a friend who helps us see more clearly, as one who makes even "ungainly things" beautiful.

Work Cited

Wallace, Robert. *Writing Poems.* Boston: Little, Brown, 1982.

From English Journal, *January 1988, 94–97*

7 Opulence to Decadence:
The Outsiders and *Less Than Zero*

Ellen A. Seay

"The times, they are a-changin'." Bob Dylan sang it back in the 1960s, and it was a particularly applicable message in those turbulent times. Adolescent literature has ridden the crest of change in the last twenty years, just like adult fiction. Fiction for juveniles no longer gives us virginal Sally worrying about whether or not John will give her his class ring at the senior prom. It was fun and it was mindless, and certainly several generations of boys and girls were not harmed by what they read. Life in general was wonderful if you worked hard, studied hard, and drank your milk. The rewards of these endeavors were a good job, a good spouse, nice children, a frame house, a dog, and a paneled station wagon. What more could any nice, young, white, middle-class American teenager want?

What they wanted, eventually, was reality. And they got it. Of course, there are those who will argue that they have gotten too much, too soon. But, unquestionably, adolescent fiction has caught up with the adult demand for truth in literature.

What still varies isn't so much the telling, but what is being told. Surely S. E. Hinton's adolescent classic *The Outsiders* (New York: Viking, 1967) has as much to say about the inherent good in teens as Bret Easton Ellis' recently published *Less Than Zero* (New York: Simon and Schuster, 1985) has to say about all that is bad. While *The Outsiders* is uplifting and positive despite tragic occurrences, the nihilistic *Less Than Zero* offers only the truth of the no hope/no solution Southern California teens of the late 1980s. Despite vast differences between the books, both have been controversial in their own times and both are eerily effective and moving in their own ways.

Briefly, *Zero* chronicles the reentry of Clay, a freshman at a small Ivy League college, into the fast-paced California lifestyle he has left behind. Clay spends his Christmas vacation reexperiencing this lifestyle and examining his place in it.

On the surface, there seems to be little in common between the two books. *The Outsiders* was written twenty years ago by then sixteen-year-old S. E. Hinton. It dealt with the split between the high school social classes in Tulsa, Oklahoma. *Less Than Zero*, written by twenty-year-old Ellis, then a Bennington College undergraduate, takes place in 1986. *Zero*, which is rapidly gathering a cult following, deals with the pursuit of something, anything, meaningful by the eighteen- and nineteen-year-old children of the idly rich of Los Angeles and surrounding affluent areas. The main characters in *The Outsiders* are poor and on the lower end of the financial and social scale, while their counterparts in *Less Than Zero* define the top of that same scale. The "greasers" in Hinton's novel have nothing but their pride and their desires. Their enemies are the "Socs," the financially well-off teens who live on the other side of town and torment them as a pastime. Ellis's characters have all that one could financially desire: the best cars, the best bars, the best clothes, the best music, the best drugs. Their enemies aren't the poor—they are themselves.

Both stories deal with violence, but it is a different kind of violence. In *The Outsiders*, Ponyboy and Johnny flee into the country when Johnny stabs and kills Bob in self-defense. The inevitable gang fight is set up to settle the score. The characters in Hinton's novel deal in various levels of physical violence to compensate for their lack of things: lack of respect, lack of money, lack of stature, lack of a visibly bright future. They fight in their various ways: Two-Bit's pride and joy is a fancy black-handled switchblade; Steve and Darry are both into building their physiques; Tim Shepard and his gang slash tires and beat up people for the hell of it; and Dallas rolls drunks, fights, and in the end, dies after sticking up a store in frustration and rage. The message in some way seems to be that those who live by violence will die by it in the same degree.

But while violence in *The Outsiders* is intensely real in its physical manifestations, the violence in *Less Than Zero*, although not physical, is equally devastating. We are used to dealing with violence as a physical concept: beatings, shootings, stabbings, or other bodily damage. But what about the violence to one's mind? Seemingly, in the twenty years between the two novels, the violence has turned inward.

The mental violence of *Less Than Zero* occurs for a variety of reasons. What is questionable is whether it occurs because of outside influences or whether the characters, in their search for excitement and stimulation, do it to themselves. The main character, Clay, forces himself in horror and fascination to watch his childhood friend, Julian, willingly commit a number of homosexual acts for money. Society generally views homosexuality negatively as something of a perversion. Yet Clay's quest for excitement has led him to cast aside societal mores, and he enters into a horror world, a counter world to what society sees as normal. He sleeps with an acquaintance, Griffin, and is seemingly unaffected by the incident. He snorts an abundance of cocaine and attends parties where his friends are in some way or another messed up. Their problems have no meaning for him, and his life is equally meaningless to his friends. They don't question him about anything other than surface matters unless he appears to be breaking out of the quest-for-desire mold that they all live in.

All this contributes to a collapse within Clay's mind. Everything around him is opulent, and yet decadent, with outside influences no doubt contributing to his downfall. The cocaine, the fancy cars, the beautiful and rich males and females, the free sex, and the endless supply of money that can purchase all of the above are the weapons that he turns upon himself. In the midst of absolute riches, he can find nothing worth thinking about or working for. The opulence does its violence upon him in that he becomes one of the mindless. Apparently, this is the only way he can save himself.

But ultimately, he does have control. In the end, his abuse of all around him is his own choice. The violence that results within his mind kills part of him, just as surely as the policeman's bullet kills Dallas Winston. The two of them are alike in that the violence done to them comes from outside factors. And yet both of them willingly brought it upon themselves in a desperate effort to gain control, in some way, of their lives.

While the differences between these two books are obvious, there are many subtle ways that they are alike. Both deal with an unwanted faction of society. The greasers are loved by no one but their own and are generally feared and despised. While abusing them and beating them up, the Socs fear the greasers, as do the nurses in the hospital and the newspapermen who cover Johnny and Ponyboy's story. While the other factions of society reject the greasers, the rejection of the teens in *Less Than Zero* is a bit more subliminal. Author Ellis never comes out and says that they are hated, or despised. If anything, they are probably idolized by the less fortunate who wish they were as well off.

Yet the rejection and the labeling of these characters as an unwanted faction of society is there. It is not the other characters in the story who do the rejecting; it is the reader. We reject them as worthless because of their self-absorption. We reject them because of the almost nonhuman way that they deal with each other and the world. Their lack of feelings and emotions repels us. And we are particularly critical of them because they have everything; the world is an open door, and they have all of the keys. Yet they wallow in their pettiness and never use the opportunities that they have had handed to them to do anything that could be called ethically worthwhile.

There is a marked absence of parenting as we know it in both *The Outsiders* and *Less Than Zero*. In Hinton's novel, the parents are apparently dead, nonexistent, or not around. But Darry acts as a sort of parent for Ponyboy and Soda after their parents are killed in an auto accident. He sacrifices college opportunities so that he may work and keep what is left of his family together. He monitors Ponyboy's reading material and is constantly on him about his schoolwork. He sets curfews and even tries to get Soda and Ponyboy to eat right. Yet Darry is not the parent. If anything, he is the model of what most teenagers want: a parent who is both strict and understanding. He exhibits parental ways, yet he is a friend as well. By most teenagers' standards, parents cannot be friends.

In *Less Than Zero* there are parents, but for all practical purposes, there might as well not be any. Their function in the lives of their children seems to be limited to providing the necessities of life: food, shelter, cable TV. They are consumed in their own lives and what attention they pay to their children is almost perfunctory. Clay's father asks him what he wants for Christmas: how about renewing his subscription to *Variety*? As a substitute for real conversation, these parents buy their children material things because they believe this is all that is demanded or required of them. One of Clay's friends, Kim, never seems to know where her mother is and finds out by reading the gossip columns in some of the trade rags. She isn't overly concerned; she only wants to know so that she will be able to answer the question when someone asks her.

Both of these books are striking examples of adolescent literature and the extremes to which it has gone. Both tell effective and haunting stories. Both make points that are well taken and succeed in opening our eyes. But the similarities end there.

Hinton's novel contains no sex, no graphic physical violence, and no bad or offensive language. Yet the novel was a success without those elements and is considered a minor teenage classic. The time in which it was written may have dictated that these elements not be contained in the book; but even so, it really doesn't need them to succeed. Adding sex, gore and bad language would have changed the scope and tone of *The Outsiders* and probably would have focused unnecessary attention on those aspects. If anything, their inclusion in the story may have taken away from it. In the same way, taking out the sex, gore, and language in *Less Than Zero* would have severely diminished the message. It is devastating because of the dealings with those very things, and the characters are what they are because of their deep involvement in all of these. Their dealings with the dark side of life are what make them, and the story, what it is.

What can be learned from *Less Than Zero* far outweighs the inclusion of sex, violence, homosexuality, drug abuse, and all the other dark elements that make up the book. Few readers want to experience the anguish of Clay, trapped in an exclusive *Alice in Wonderland* setting. What they want to do is wish that he could see beyond his gilded cage and take advantage of the opportunities that he has. They learn by example what is good and what is bad. There will be a few students who will wish that they had a Jag, all the coke in the world, great clothes, and sex with whomever and whenever they want. After all, we've all been taught to work to be rich and if we do so, the rewards will be ours. But those who read further will find that the payoff is not without a price. The price is one's soul, and, for Clay, the payment is due.

The Hinton book is a classic because it deals with the basic tenets of the human spirit: good and evil. While society frowns upon Ponyboy, Dallas, and the rest of the greasers, we as readers see that they have much to offer that is positive. Compared to Clay and his cohorts, Ponyboy and the greasers have much. They have a brotherhood, a unity amongst their own for which they are willing to fight. They take care of and are concerned about each other. They are willing to make sacrifices. Dallas gives Johnny and Pony a gun, even though it could mean jail for him. He takes the heat from the police and spends a night in jail so that the police will look elsewhere for the fugitives. Darry gives up his dreams of college to support his brothers. Dallas, although unable to express it, wants Johnny to have a better life than he did. He doesn't want Johnny to be hurt by the world and become as hardened to it as he has.

The spirituality of *Less Than Zero* is equally unifying, but only in a surface way. All of the people around Clay are bound by a like desire to push life to the edge in a blind search for anything vaguely interesting. They depend on each other for drugs, sex, gossip, and rides home. However, this common bond isn't anything that any are willing, like Dallas and Darry in *The Outsiders,* to fight for. Their concerns center around their own problems and never seem to extend to their friends. Nowhere in the book is this better displayed than in a scene where Clay and Kim seek out an anorexic friend at Kim's New Year's Eve party and find her distraught and shooting up heroin in Kim's back bedroom.

Instead of trying to save her by talking her out of it, they sit by and watch, spellbound, while she plays drug roulette.

The sacrifices that Clay and his friends are willing to make have little to do with caring about their fellow humans. As a matter of fact, they almost fall to the level of human sacrifices, as shown by their actions and lackadaisical attitude towards others. Clay finds Rip and Spin amusing themselves by having sex with a twelve-year-old girl who has sold herself to them in exchange for drugs. While Clay watches in horror and fascination, Spin shoots her up and then has sex with her. No one seems to care, including the apparently willing victim, who lies there throughout in a drug-induced stupor.

What Hinton wants to say in *The Outsiders* far transcends the realistic actions of the characters. For this reason, the novel is timeless. In the same sense, *Less Than Zero* could be symbolic of an isolated element of teenage society. The violence, gore, and sex are necessary because of their direct influence upon the characters.

We are fortunate to live in a society where teenagers can be exposed to all facets of life through literature. Some would vehemently disagree, and perhaps they have valid points. Is it necessary for students to read about the almost evil, almost diabolical lifestyles of Clay and his friends? The questions that educators and parents alike need to ask are not whether it is necessary, but whether the situations exist. If they do, then teens have the right to read about them. And in so doing, maybe learn a lesson.

From English Journal, *October 1987, 69–72*

8 Foreign Affairs: Contact Literature in English

Michael Spooner

> We cannot write like the English. . . . We cannot write *only* as Indians. . . . Our method of expression therefore has to be a dialect which will some day prove to be as distinctive and colorful as the Irish and the American.
>
> —Raja Rao (viii)

English is now a world language. Linguists have compared the role of modern English to the Latin of the Late Roman Empire and to the historic importance of Sanskrit throughout the South Asian subcontinent. At first largely through the (often unwelcome) agency of the British Empire, and more recently through the influence of industry, aviation, the information age, and attendant technologies. English has come to play a significant role in cultures in which it is not indigenous. These cultures include India and the rest of South Asia, East and West Africa, the Caribbean, the Philippines, many Asian countries, and, arguably, American and Canadian Indian nations.

As English becomes institutionalized in nations that do not share its Western cultural traditions, the language is broadening. Contact with non-Western cultures and languages calls English into service to express a new array of linguistic and cultural functions. The English produced in new contexts naturally takes on the "flavor" of its surroundings, delivering a blend of native and Western linguistic features, semantic and pragmatic qualities, literary heritages, and the like.

Braj B. Kachru has analyzed the relationships among the "Englishes" of what he calls the "Inner Circle" (native English cultures) and the "Outer Circle" (non-native English cultures). Since the latter varieties of English—called nativized—are produced by the contact between the language, the culture, and surrounding languages, so the literatures written in those varieties are often called "contact literatures." (The term is also applied to creative writing in nativized varieties of other languages—African French, for example.)

Contact literature in English is of considerable interest, then, to a number of academic disciplines, including sociolinguistics, comparative literature, semiotics, reader-response theory, and ESL. These works also provide a trove of material for the mainstream English classroom. For many English teachers, however, contact literature poses a number of questions.

Is It Credible Literature?

It's more than a question of taste. Linguists, teachers, general readers, and skeptics alike wonder if it is truly possible in a given language adequately to represent the experience, thought, or discourse style of a culture not native to that language. Ronald Blaber briefly but carefully uncovers the semiotic ground that underlies this question.

Drawing on the terminology of semioticians Lotman and Eco, Blaber describes the special predicament of the creative writer in a second language. To get at a central issue in the writing of contact literature, Blaber distinguishes between (1) the personal or cultural *content* of a text, and (2) the *conventions* of language—syntax, lexicon, and so forth (i.e., the formal dimension through which that content is presented).

The formal dimension provides information in terms of what Lotman calls a "primary modeling system," while the cultural dimension—philosophy, attitudes, aesthetics—constitutes a "secondary modeling system." These systems merge within the text to give a work its meaning. In Lotman's view, the primary system (formal) dominates the secondary system (cultural); thus, writers of contact literature inevitably frustrate themselves, trapped (though by choice) within a language that is alien to their culture. "Essentially," Blaber says, "this is a variation of the Whorf-Sapir hypothesis."

More than a matter of taste, then, the question addresses the *viability* of contact literature from a semiotic perspective. Won't such literature be ineffective since so much of the non-English culture will be inexpressible in English?

To this, the writers answer a resounding "no." Chinua Achebe, noted Nigerian poet and fictionist, says this:

> I feel the English language will be able to carry the weight of my experience. But it will have to be a new English, still in full communion with its ancestral home, but altered to suit its new African surroundings. . . . The price a world language must be prepared to pay is submission to many different kinds of use. (82)

K. S. Narayana Rao agrees:

> Expressions in the original language acquire a new sense in English, or what is perfectly sensible in one language becomes illogical when put in another. For the Indian writing in English, the challenge is to bend it to suit the needs to convey Indian sensibility. (160)

In other words, these writers turn the semiotic objection on its head. They suggest that the cultural material (Lotman's secondary modeling system) will stretch or reshape the expressive possibilities of the language (primary modeling system). One need only remember the variations in the English used by native speakers—compare the American with the Irish—to see this is plausible.

Is This Really English?

One of the most important current issues in US education as noted by the NCTE Commission on the English Language is the misunderstanding and mistrust of language variation by teachers as well as the public (Schuster). The impetus behind the "English Only" movement and much of the back-to-basics energy of education reformers seems to spring from a confidence that what we call "Standard English" is somehow above the reach of variation.

However, a glance at the history of English in America, even simply at historical documents, reminds us that the dialect called standard has changed markedly over time. "Fourscore and seven years," for example, became a conspicuously nonstandard construction after a mere generation or two. Even among speakers of grammatically "standard" English today, neologisms ("prioritize"), slang ("yuppie"), and loan words from other languages ("cassette") invade the American lexicon regularly. And of course, regional pronunciations in America compete for acceptance and prestige. Comparing American usage, lexicon, and "accent" with Canadian, Australian, English, and Irish reveals what a wide range of variation is tolerable among native speakers of a single language.

Once we acknowledge that variation is a constant feature of "standard" dialects, we can more easily see the rationale for Raja Rao's point of view in the epigraph to this article. This perspective allows us (1) to admit the English that Americans write is as much a product of language contact, physical environment, history, and development as any other variety of English, and (2) to approach the newer varieties of written English—like Indian and African English—with the interest and respect we accord established varieties—like Irish and American English.

The Sound of English

> Then the police inspector saunters up to the Skefflington gate, and he opens it and one coolie and two coolies and three coolies come out, their faces dark as mops and their blue skin black under the clouded heavens, and perspiration flows down their bodies and their eyes seem fixed to the earth—one coolie and two coolies and three coolies and four and five come out, their eyes fixed to the earth, their stomachs black and clammy and bulging, and they march toward the toddy booth; and then suddenly more coolies come out, more and more and more like clogged bullocks. (Rao 137)

According to S. N. Sridhar, when Rao sets out to bend English to convey Indian sensibility in this kind of passage, he creates an almost endless chain of coordinations. The result is a very effective facsimile of the "breathless" cadences of Kannada, a South Asian language which typically multiplies participial clauses.

Authors use other devices as well to convey in English the sound and flavor of their native culture. Sridhar lists the following common examples from Indian English writers:

> *the verbless sentence*—"Don't touch. Not completely dry yet." (Narayan)
>
> *the subjectless sentence*—"When a man says 'I love you' it sounds mechanical. . . . Perhaps credible in Western society, but sounds silly in ours." (Narayan)
>
> *questions without inversion*—"Brother, you are with me?" (R. Rao)
>
> *left and right dislocation*—"And he can sing too, can Jayaramachar." (R. Rao)

Kachru details other experiments in style and discourse which likewise transform English to create the sensibility of other non-English, "Outer Circle" cultures.

How Does It Work in the Classroom?

Since writers of contact literature necessarily draw from a double repertoire of literary traditions, a critical approach that accommodates only Western tradition would not be productive in the classroom.

Edwin Thumboo details a theoretical perspective which accounts for both the non-English and the English (i.e., Western) literary "ecology." Each, he says, "has powerful traditions marked by particular linguistic, literary, and aesthetic preoccupations," and he argues that the connections between the two need to be addressed.

As the writer's native culture "bends" the formal conventions of Western English, it also requires readers to bend their expectations of both what is tolerable formally and what is predictable culturally in English. Jill May suggests that a good way to start in the classroom is to discuss the culture which will be encountered in the literature. Particular attention to students' linguistic and cultural biases is warranted, including possible pretesting of cultural knowledge, class discussion of customs, history, myths, and languages within the culture.

The experience of reading contact literature for the first time can seem quite an exotic one, both linguistically and culturally, eliciting important exploratory responses from students. For this reason, a pedagogy grounded in reader-response theory or transactional criticism seems especially useful. Probst maintains that debate focusing on discovering the "right" conclusion is not appropriate in the literature classroom. Instead, he says, teachers face a challenging but rewarding task: "encouraging students to articulate responses, examine their origins in the text and in other experiences, reflect upon them, and analyze them. . . . Discussions should encourage students not to win but to clarify and refine."

The rise of contact literature in English provides an opportunity to study in a unique way the literary efforts of international writers, and at the same time to observe the vital process of language change. This change is of special interest to English teachers and students, since it is our language we are observing, and since the development it undergoes will make it a more sensitive and authentic vehicle for creative expression of consciousness in non-Western cultures.

For more information on contact literature, consult the ERIC database using the descriptors Literature Appreciation, Nonstandard Dialects, World Literature, African Literature, American Indian Literature, Sociolinguistics, Literature Programs, Curriculum Enrichment.

Works Cited

Achebe, Chinua. "The African Writer and the English Language." *Morning Yet on Creation Day*. New York: Anchor, 1976.

Blaber, Ronald L. "The More We Read: Contact Literature and the Reader." *Cultural Reflections: Papers from the Project Contact Literature in Cross-National Perspective.* Ed. Paul Sharrad. Honolulu: Hawaii U, 1981.

Kachru, Braj B. "The Bilingual's Creativity: Discoursal and Stylistic Strategies in Contact Literatures in English." *Studies in the Linguistic Sciences.* 13.2 (1983): 37–55.

———. "Standards, Codification, and Sociolinguistic Realism: The English Language in the Outer Circle." *English in the World.* Ed. Randolph Quirk and Henry Widdowson. Cambridge: Cambridge UP, 1985.

May, Jill. "To Think Anew: Native American Indian Literature and Children's Attitudes." *The Reading Teacher.* 36.8 (1983): 790–94.

Narayan, R. K. *The Painter of Signs.* New York: Viking, 1976.

Probst, Robert. "Transactional Theory in the Teaching of Literature." ERIC Digest, 1987.

Rao, K. S. Narayana. "The Untranslated Translation and Aesthetic Consequences: Indian Fiction in English." *Expression Communication and Experience.* Ed. R. G. Popperwell. London: The Modern Humanities Research Association, 1973.

Rao, Raja. *Kanthapura.* London: Oxford UP, 1943.

Schuster, Charles, and others. "Trends and Issues in English Instruction, 1987—Seven Summaries." CS 210 417

Sridhar, S. N. "Non-native English Literatures: Context and Relevance." *The Other Tongue: English Across Cultures.* Ed. Braj B. Kachru. Oxford: Pergamon Institute of English, 1982.

Thumboo, Edwin. "Twin Perspectives and Multi-Ecosystems: Tradition for a Commonwealth Writer." *World Englishes.* 4.2 (1985): 213–22.

Getting Started: Readings in Contact Literature

Listed below are some examples of contact literature. Any of these titles might serve as a good starting point for teachers or students. Publisher information is for the most recent paperback edition.

Achebe, Chinua. (Nigeria) *Things Fall Apart.* New York: Fawcett, 1978.

The tragedy of Okonkwo, an Ibo tribesman, who is trapped between the traditional values of his tribe and the coming of white Christian missionaries.

Anand, Mulk Raj. (India) *Untouchable.* New York: Ind.-US Inc., 1983.

One day in the life of Bakha, a street sweeper and member of India's lowest caste.

Naipaul, V. S. (Trinidad) *A House for Mr. Biswas.* New York: Random, 1984.

The life story of one Mr. Biswas that is both a portrait of an "ordinary" man and a rich evocation of the people and places of Trinidad.

Narayan, R. K. (India) *Under the Banyan Tree and Other Stories.* New York: Penguin, 1985.

A selection of Narayan's stories from the last forty years, populated with a motley cast of characters and written with great grace and wit. Narayan's tales have been compared to those of Dickens and O. Henry.

Ndebele, Njabulo. (South Africa) *Fools and Other Stories.* New York: Readers International, 1986.

Stories of life in South Africa's black townships, most of which focus on children or adolescents. Ndebele is one of the important new writers emerging from South Africa.

Soyinka, Wole. (Nigeria) *Ake: The Years of Childhood.* New York: Random, 1983.

An autobiography of the Nobel Prize-winning Nigerian's first eleven years that provides a vivid picture of growing up in a small town in western Nigeria in the 1930s.

From English Journal, *November 1987, 45–48*

9 Celebrating the Black Female Self: Zola Neale Hurston's American Classic

Julie Roemer

Alice Walker tells a story about the time Zola Neale Hurston attended a party honoring the recipients of a young playwrights' award (1979, *I Love Myself When I Am Laughing . . .*, Old Westbury, NY: Feminist). Hurston, at that time a recent Barnard graduate, had received second prize for her first published work, a play entitled *Color Struck*. She arrived at the reception fashionably late, paused dramatically in the doorway, tossed her scarf around her throat, and sang out at the top of her voice, "Color-r-r Str-r-ruck!!"

Twelve years later, in 1937, Hurston published *Their Eyes Were Watching God* (1978, Urbana: U of Illinois P), a novel grounded in this same celebration of the self—specifically, of the black female self. The hero, Janie Mae Crawford, is a young black woman living in the post-World War I rural South. Her long, and ultimately successful, struggle for her authentic self compels her to confront and overcome a gauntlet of limiting expectations of "Whut a woman oughta be and to do" (Hurston 31). Hurston structures Janie's story as a classic hero's quest, transcribed to the feminine. Janie's geography is principally an inner one; the obstacles in her path are the loud voices of others which drown out the sound of her own inner voice.

The Importance of Reading Female

Judith Fetterley (1978, *The Resisting Reader: A Feminist Approach to American Fiction*, Bloomington: Indiana UP) has pointed out that reading only from the canon of traditional classics of English and American literature may maneuver a young woman into identifying against herself—or into adopting a "male" perspective about women characters. Equally disturbing is Tillie Olsen's suggestion (1978, *Silences*, New York: Delta/Seymour Lawrence) that, failing to see her own experiences—both inner and outer—reflected accurately in literature, a young woman may begin to sense that there is something wrong with her experiences. If she has been inclined to write, she may lose confidence that she has something of value to say and remain silent.

Believing these things, largely because they shed much light on my own experience, I approached teaching, hoping to give better than I had received. I cherished among my goals increasing the sensitivity of my students to gender issues in literature and offering them—both young women and men—central images of women that are both real and positive.

As a first-year teacher, I had the exceptional luck to receive the support of my department in pioneering *Their Eyes Were Watching God* in my college-prep, junior English classes. At the end of that year, our district added the novel to the list of recommended core books for the eleventh grade. *Their Eyes Were Watching God* is uniquely well suited for the high-school curriculum. Its compelling thematic concerns riveted my students' attention, Hurston's stunning narration and poetic rendering of southern black speech refreshed their literary eyes and hearts, and her complex but accessible symbolic structure offered them ample opportunity for challenging interpretive work.

The Search for Far Horizon

Janie Mae Crawford's Nanny is an ex-slave who preaches "a great sermon about colored women sittin' on high" as the desirable alternative to her own use as a "work-ox and a brood sow" (Hurston 31). Nanny senses her approaching death and forces sixteen-year-old Janie into a loveless marriage to a man with some economic means but no poetry in his soul. Janie, however, has already experienced the first stirrings of sexual and spiritual desire.

> She was stretched on her back beneath the pear tree soaking in the alto chant of the visiting bees, the gold of the sun and the panting breath of the breeze when the inaudible voice of it all came to her. She saw a dust-bearing bee sink into the sanctum of a bloom; the thousand sister-calyxes arch to meet the love embrace and the ecstatic shiver of the tree from root to tiniest branch creaming in every blossom and frothing with delight. So this was a marriage! She had been summoned to behold revelation. Then Janie felt a pain remorseless sweet that left her limp and languid. (Hurston 24)

Janie quickly realizes that her husband "desecrates the pear tree," and after the death of her Nanny, she takes her first opportunity to run for far horizon.

Unfortunately, her ticket to ride is Jody Starks, a man with ambitions to be the first black mayor of the first all-black town, who has very definite ideas about "Mrs. Mayor Starks" and her role. He batters Janie against the rock of her privileges, forces her to cover her luxuriant hair, and forbids her to participate in the community storytelling sessions. The first time he strikes her, Janie

> stood where he left her for unmeasured time and thought. She stood there until something fell off the shelf inside her. Then she went inside there to see what it was. It was her image of Jody tumbled down and shattered. . . . She had no more blossomy openings dusting pollen over her man, neither any glistening young fruit where the petals used to be. She found that she had a host of thoughts she had never let Jody know about. . . . She had an inside and an outside now and suddenly she knew how not to mix them. (Hurston 113)

Janie's awareness of the rift between her inner and outer lives leads her to her greatest spiritual challenge—how to reconcile the two and live an authentic life, not the life prescribed for her by others, particularly her husbands. After Jody's death, it appears that Janie may have healed the rift and learned to live for herself. To the dismay of her community, she marries Vergible "Tea Cake" Woods, a man considerably younger, darker, and poorer than she.

Colorism Blights the Pear Tree

In many ways, Janie and Tea Cake's relationship is a breathtaking example of Janie's revelation under the pear tree: sensual, playful, mutually enriching. They leave Eatonville, travel deep into the Florida Everglades, and make their living picking beans in a wild, fertile environment known as the Muck. Here Janie lets her hair flow, willingly dons overalls to work beside Tea Cake in the fields, and tells stories at community gatherings. In fact, the power of Janie and Tea Cake's love and romance makes Hurston's subsequent narrative choices extremely provocative and underscores her daring.

Janie is a mulatta. Because she places so much importance in inner realities, her long, wavy hair and coffee-and-cream complexion matter little to her. They are consistently, however, standards by which other people judge her. On the Muck, Janie meets Mrs. Turner, who articulates this standard.

> Ah can't stand black niggers. Ah don't blame de white folks from hatin' 'em cause ah can't stand 'em mahself. 'Nother thing, Ah hates

> tuh see folks lak me and you mixed up wid 'em. Us oughta class off
> . . . . If it wuzn't for so many black folks it wouldn't be no race
> problem. De white folks would take us in wid 'em. De black ones is
> holdin' us back. (Hurston 210)

Janie is baffled by this internalized race hatred—or colorism—but
Tea Cake is infected. With no provocation in her behavior—in fact, to
the contrary—he becomes increasingly insecure about Janie's love for
him. Why, in his twisted reasoning, would a light black woman choose
a dark black man? When Mrs. Turner's light-skinned brother visits the
Muck, Tea Cake beats Janie to reassure himself in possession. A painful
exchange between Tea Cake and a friend follows in which they compare
the relative human merits of a "high time woman" (light-skinned) and
a "rusty black woman" (dark-skinned).

> "Tea Cake, you sho is a lucky man," Sop de Bottom told him. "Uh
> person can see every place you hit her. Ah bet she never raised her
> hand tuh hit yuh back, neither. Take some uh dese ol' rusty black
> women and dey would fight yuh all night long and next day nobody
> couldn't tell you ever hit 'em." (Hurston 219)

About this experience Janie maintains an eloquent silence. Eventually,
a fatal fever snaps Tea Cake's mind. His jealousy overwhelms him, and
he fires his shotgun at Janie. She must shoot him in self-defense or die,
a victim of his colorist stereotyping and lack of belief in her inner truth.
She chooses to live.

At her trial, Janie's only weapon in her own defense is her now-
strong voice, articulating her true self. She succeeds in representing her
"inside" in the "outside" world and is acquitted. Back at home, she
relates her whole story to her best friend Phoeby, encourages Phoeby to
repeat her story to the community, and urges everyone to live from the
inside out. Now alone, although still sensual and self-assured, she
wraps herself in her memories, and Phoeby hurries off into the
gathering darkness.

Reading and Writing beyond the Ending

In a literature—and a world—in which women are often drawn (and
drawn in!) by the fantasies of others, Janie's fierce and loving choice for
herself is both a shock and an inspiration. The implications can
reverberate for days in a classroom—or a life. Some of my students
rebelled. They simply refused to read or write beyond the "happily-ever-
after" ending of Janie and Tea Cake's love affair and ignored the last

crucial sequences of the novel. Concluding her essay on the development of Janie's sexuality, Megan writes,

> I am happy that Janie finally found Tea Cake and happiness. Tea Cake was Janie's fulfillment mentally and spiritually. I hope one day that I will find a man who will satisfy all of my needs.

Or from Jeff,

> I found the novel a splendid look at the real world from the eyes of a woman. Janie found fulfillment with a liberal-minded man.

Carrie, however, was able to conclude,

> As the themes of growing maturity and the desire to find love develop, Janie is engaged in three marriages. She learns a little more with each one. The third results in her own personal satisfaction, even after the death of her husband. Janie gains the self-knowledge she needs to find happiness within herself.

Shannon examined the use of the pear tree as a symbol of sexual and spiritual fulfillment.

> Unfortunately, Janie's pear tree does not give her sweet fruit forever. It actually withers and dries up with the death of Tea Cake. But Janie has already figured out how to live for herself, and despite Tea Cake's death she will forever have an inner peace concerning the pear tree.

Andy wrote,

> [Janie] is determined to be her own master. Her decisions and choices completely defy the images . . . for the ordinary black woman to follow. Her repudiation of the images leads to the creation of a human being.

Erin projected Hurston—and I believe herself—into Janie's struggle.

> Zora must have identified with the struggles Janie lived through. By seeing the struggle on paper Zora was able to identify and deal with them in her own life.

That the impassioned journey of a black woman through love and heartbreak toward self-definition can result in student writing and thinking like this is, for me, the source of deep gratification and hope. Beyond imparting a sheer love of the words themselves, I hope that reading *Their Eyes Were Watching God* and "seeing the struggle on paper" will stretch my students' own horizons of possibility.

From English Journal, *November 1989, 70–72*

10 Neighborhoods: Maya Angelou's "Harlem Hopscotch"

Sister J. Eleanor Mayer, IHM

Harlem Hopscotch

One foot down, then hop! It's hot.
    Good things for the ones that's got.
Another jump, now to the left.
    Everybody for hisself.

In the air, now both feet down.
    Since you black, don't stick around.
Food is gone, the rent is due,
    Curse and cry and then jump two.

All the people out of work,
    Hold for three, then twist and jerk.
Cross the line, they count you out.
    That's what's hopping's all about.

Both feet flat, the game is done.
They think I lost. I think I won.*

—Maya Angelou

The first time my class and I encountered "Harlem Hopscotch" it was totally by accident. We were viewing a videocassette of the series Bill Moyers had done on *Creativity* for public television, in which he interviewed Maya Angelou as his first subject. Toward the end of the segment, Angelou visited a classroom of upper elementary or junior-high students to talk with them about success—her actual and their potential achievement of it. At the end of the sharing, she recited (although her presentation is so much more drama than recital) the poem "Harlem Hopscotch," transforming the last line into "They say you lost. I think you won."

The tape ended. My classroom full of senior track-one, upper-Main-Line girls sat at first in perfect stillness. Finally, one girl broke the quiet,

---

*"Harlem Hopscotch," by Maya Angelou. Reprinted by permission of Hirt Music, Inc. c/o G.W. Purcell Assoc., 964 2nd Ave., New York, NY 10022.

"We have a few minutes, Sister. Just play the part with the poem back again. Let us see it." Her request became unanimous. So I replayed and we rewatched.

It took me almost a month of library searching and reading of Angelou's anthologies to find the text of "Harlem Hopscotch," but I knew the discovery would be worth the looking. Never had I seen students take so naturally to a poem or the rendition of one.

The day I brought the copy in, the class recognized it immediately. "It's the poem from the movie," one girl said with the air of opening a Christmas present. "Where did you find it?" asked another. I told them of my library journeys, of the help I had received from reference librarians, and my readings in Angelou's life and works. Then we began to enter into the world of "Harlem Hopscotch." At first volunteers read it. Several tried to recapture the enthusiasm, the rhythm that Angelou had delivered on the film. One girl, Ellen—always the enthusiast— asked if a group could work up a "rap" for the next day. I told them to go for it and they did, with choral movement and gesture that would put a modern Sophocles to shame.

After the many interpretive readings, we talked about the poem as a whole. First, I asked, "What is it about?" "It's about a neighborhood," said Luci, "the black inner city of New York." Had any of them ever been there? It seemed many had and had stories to tell. One narrated her brother's experience around Columbia University, of stripped tires, and great neighbors, of being taunted with names like "Mayonnaise" from upper story windows. Christine told of getting lost in the area and of a policeman's telling her and her friend to lock the doors and not stop even for red lights. Some compared it to the areas around inner-city Philadelphia with which they were more familiar. A few recounted fright stories—late at night, lost and alone, surrounded by boarded-up or burned-out buildings. Others shared good experiences—help received when they had a flat, directions given, college friends who knew really great people who lived in these "harlems" and looked out for each other and for "those who belonged."

Then Heather said, "But I don't think this poem is just about a neighborhood. It's about life . . . all levels of life." That led us to the concept of the extended metaphor, the simple childhood play translated into the complex game of life. So we started to analyze it, to take note of the steps in the hopscotch to see what they meant for us. We asked, "Why did Angelou use the words she did?" Sheila found the word "hot" in the first line very evocative. She described the small child she imagined playing the game on summer's sizzling streets with bare feet slapping against the asphalt: the only way to survive in such conditions is to move. Is that how Angelou was cautioning her reader? was warning us? Another girl saw the "hot" as capturing the emotion of the game. "You start playing and you're into it. It doesn't matter that your mother is sitting on an old mattress in the corner of the steps or that your baby brother has nothing on but a diaper. You're playing and it is great." Is the game meant as an escape?

We watched the directions the moves traced. In line three why hop to the left? Much discussion stirred around this one word. One girl mentioned that the normal, the expected move is to the right. In a world where a person is trapped—by poverty, by the expectations of others— a person has to take the unexpected turn to win. Another brought up the connotations of left—*sinister* in Latin—and its modern associations with radical movements. She connected this to the following line (line 4) that stresses individualism. To win, to move out, sometimes the extreme might be necessary. Most loved the ending with its paradoxical twist—especially remembering Angelou's revision of it for the students in the video.

Other elements of poetry that entered into our discussion included form, language, and rhythm. It hadn't occurred to me, veteran English teacher and poetry analyzer, that Angelou was working from the traditional sonnet format until Megan noted it, calling from the left-hand corner of the room, "Isn't this a sort of sonnet? I know that it's not in iambic pentameter, but then it is supposed to be modern. It even has the Shakespearean couplet ending." That moved us to examine what rhythm it did follow. The pattern would have been difficult to trace had it not been for our having heard Angelou say it herself.

"I remember," recalled Halle, "she used the movement of the game itself. When she wanted to give the feel of coming down, as in line one, the word came down. The same thing happens at the beginning of stanza two." Another voice added that in stanza three when the deliberate pause in the game and life are marked (lines 9–10), a slowing seems to occur. "Why? How does it happen?" I asked. "The first line of that stanza draws the movement out with the word 'people' and the phrase 'out of work,' and then the next line picks up the pace again— especially when you hit the sound words 'twist' and 'jerk,'" a student ventured.

That ended the day's class and our analysis of the poem as it related to the life experiences of the people in the poem—in their words, their world, their rhythm and their images, but it did not end our experience with the poem. At the opening of the next day's work, we spent ten minutes free writing on how "Harlem Hopscotch" spoke to each of us. When they finished, those students who wanted to shared their reflections. Kara opened by relating her current adventures of applying to college. The boxes on the hopscotch square she equated with college choices, some mostly dreams, others more realizable goals. She wrote, "The final two lines represent my acceptance and the waiting being finally over. Maybe my destination isn't the most prestigious university; maybe to some it doesn't seem like much. But, I know that I've made it to the top with what I've been given."

Another girl shared an extremely personal experience of moving from affluence to "serious economic changes" due to parental sickness and family problems. She saw herself moving through "Harlem Hopscotch" like the jumper: "I have, like the player in that poem, worked through the disabilities, the setbacks and I know that I'm better for it. I have concluded that like the player and like Maya Angelou, I can take what life gives me and rise above it."

Other sharings involved expectations that come from teachers, family, self, the loss of a loved one, family separations, and daily hurts. The events and feelings were as different as each student, but on one point they all agreed. Lisa summarized it for them all: "I love this poem. It is so real."

We are still not quite done with "Harlem Hopscotch." We have begun a creative modeling, using the idea of a childhood experience as an extended metaphor for our own poems. Ideas so far range from making mud pies, to holding hands crossing the street, to bedtime stories. All these they are paralleling to life experiences. I can hardly wait to read them.

From English Journal, *September 1988, 86–88*

11 An Afrocentric Approach to Literature: Putting the Pieces Back Together

Eileen Oliver

Recently, I observed the instruction of two preservice teachers in their respective college-bound, racially mixed senior English classes. One teacher was working over Wordsworth's "Lines Composed a Few Miles above Tintern Abbey" while her languishing students sat politely, took notes appropriately, and were distracted easily as the minutes dragged. Their instructor, noting the apathy, worked harder, poring over theme and mood, tone and imagery, ironing out each word and phrase for her passive audience.

Across the hall, the other fledgling teacher was orchestrating an analytic reading of the West African "lion and rabbit" legend. Students excitedly pointed out the signifying forms that they recognized from familiar "rap" pieces. They easily picked out images and pointed to metaphoric elements. Finally, their teacher led them to a "required" poem from the text which they analyzed with great enthusiasm, first from an Afrocentric point of view and then from the more familiar Eurocentric perspective.

The lesson objectives for these two classes were similar; yet one was working and one was not. The first teacher utilized a traditional approach. The second teacher was attempting to develop in her students an awareness of the poetic conventions of a different tradition. She then compared these principles to the criteria used almost exclusively in our Western culture and demonstrated the differences in evaluation when using different criteria.

When we talk of making connections and enriching all students with the language and literature of all cultures, we should be well past the question of "why." We've already fought that battle a number of times, a number of ways. Incorporating a variety of ethnocentric positions and traditions of literature into the curriculum is not something we do as a humanitarian gesture or as a fulfillment of department, school, or district mandate. We do it because true literacy is multicultural and because it works.

We know that interest levels, identification, and relevance head the list of motivation and achievement in literature and that students develop more positive attitudes about themselves and about school when they can relate to what they read (Hornburger 1985). In her challenge to speech, language, and composition teachers, Geneva Smitherman-Donaldson (1987) points to alarming dropout rates and declining literacy and achievement levels, especially in communities with high minority populations. In light of these shocking statistics, it is time to stop focusing on less meaningful atomistic measures and evaluations and to move away from our almost exclusive use of a Eurocentric perspective when teaching literature and the language arts. We must begin to address the real needs of our students—from minority *and* dominant cultures—and adopt realistic, workable strategies to teach them.

As for the question concerning the mainstreaming of ethnic literature versus its treatment in separate courses, both choices are correct. Students often study Shakespeare or Chaucer or Romanticism, and the like in survey classes and also pursue these areas of specialization in more concentrated classes. Accordingly, great literature written by minority writers should be taught as great literature, *and* ethnic literatures can also be taught in "special studies" (Robinson 1985). For example, while James Baldwin should always be considered a major writer in any contemporary American literature course, his works can also be studied more thoroughly in classes covering black literature, ethnic literature, or James Baldwin's literature.

"The black experience" has as much a place in the history of this country as the rise of the working class, the development of the two-party system, or the US involvement in the world wars. The problem, then, is not that ethnic concerns are not in the mainstream of our country's identity; it is, instead, that we have denied these issues for so long that they have been lost in our curriculum! To present accurate information to our students, we must acknowledge these deficiencies in background and put the material back where it belongs!

In *The Afrocentric Idea*, Molefi Asante (1987) argues against the Eurocentric ideology "that masquerades as a universal philosophy, linguistics, psychology, education, anthropology, and history." He suggests "taking the globe and turning it over so that we see all the possibilities of a world where Africa, for example, is subject and not object . . ." (3). This proposes a particularly interesting conceptual perspective for English teachers trained primarily in Western, not world, view.

Curriculum planners must recognize that black studies, indeed all ethnic studies, are interdisciplinary and should be incorporated into all

areas of learning. Asante points out that the "inability of the majority
. . . to think beyond Eurocentric ideals" has long been a hindrance to the
study of blacks in history. Excluding an Ellington from a music course,
a Du Bois from history, or a Fanon or King from philosophy reflects an
exclusivity which deprives us of a true picture in each discipline (58).
Bypassing the Black Power movement of the sixties which gave the
impetus for so many other causes and self-discoveries in the modern
world gives us and our students a false perception of reality (Asante
1987; Bennett 1986; Smitherman-Donaldson 1987).

In "Western Civilization," we do not teach the Egyptian *The
Coming Forth by Day* as the precursor and model for the writers of the
Torah, the Koran, and possibly the Bhagavad-Gita. Nor do our history
books represent the Egyptian and Nubian civilizations as formulators
of Greek and Roman thought (Asante 1987). These examples belie the
xenophobic perspective which all but eliminates a multicultural
approach to history and literature.

The Study of Black Literature

According to Darwin Turner (1985), black writers were almost all
ignored the first sixty-five years of this century; and even now, since
"minority relevance" and "cultural awareness" have become credible
goals, English teachers often treat ethnic literature in general, simplistic terms. Still not considered true art, most criticism of black literature
is devoted to a discussion of the "message" (O'Brien cited in Cook 1985),
instead of style, characterization, form, and the like. Writers are
categorized as "black writers," and major artists are often "lumped
together" with student and other novice writers. Excellent works like
Wright's *Native Son* and Hansberry's *Raisin in the Sun* become
inaccurate symbols of the total black experience. Teachers sometimes
choose popular adolescent literature which deals with social problems
encountered by black youth. But these books do not always develop the
issues clearly or portray the characters fairly, thus leaving readers with
less than favorable impressions and little positive gain from the
experience (Kiah 1985).

In asking the question "How do we exploit the power of literature to
clarify and expand the world of the reader?" Cook (1985) reminds us that
"creating relevance" is our most important tool. Turner posits that the
"universal life experience" is not confined to whites with European
ancestry. Black students are not just interested in reading "black issues."
The themes in *Romeo and Juliet, The Scarlet Letter,* and other

frequently taught "classics" have relevance to all students if taught properly. And many of the themes in black literature which also have universal relevance should be taught in the same way. He presents three suggestions for the selection and evaluation of black literature:

1. Readings should not be restricted to celebrity biographies.
2. Readers should try to see through the eyes of the author.
3. Works should be evaluated carefully with an understanding of the values of the tradition.

As teachers of language and literature, we ought to be aware of speech acts, such as sounding and the Dozens in black English, because acknowledgment of black language "as a legitimate system" facilitates fluency in students with the figurative and literary forms of what Smitherman-Donaldson calls the "language of wider communication," and "is a positive way of inviting overlap between school activities and home values" (Farr and Daniels 1986, 55). The role of alliteration and repetition in sermons and oratories helps to create the symbolic quest for freedom and traditional images of social statements in what many refer to in "the black referent." The "styling" and rhythmic codes that Asante speaks of are exemplified in the orations of Martin Luther King, Jr., and Malcolm X. In "Literature and Black Children," Hornburger offers a number of ways to enhance "creative reading" and critical thinking through discussions of and debates on literature-based questions at several different levels.

Stanford and Amin's *Black Literature for High School Students* (1978) is an excellent source for high-school teachers. Besides a historical survey which dates back to pre–Civil War writers, the authors treat traditions, goals, and objectives as well as adolescent literature and biography. Units are provided in the slave narrative and autobiography, poetry, and the short story. Examples of the connection of black literature to human relationships, myths and legends, prose nonfiction, composition, and role-playing are also presented.

Implementing the Black Aesthetic

When looking at literature, English teachers and their students must use appropriate instruments by which to judge. For example, when analyzing *Oedipus,* critics employ the classical definition—the birthright, the hubris, the action—of the tragic hero. We must also learn and teach our students to judge the characters created by black artists who come from Afrocentric traditions, not by Eurocentric models but from the styles and characteristics which most represent their works. In describing "other ways of knowing," Asante shows that the Western conceptions of thought—rationality, objectivity, progress—are inadequate for understanding the Afrocentric thinker who

> understands that the interrelationship of knowledge with cosmology, society, religion, medicine, and traditions stands alongside the interactive metaphors of discourse as principal means of achieving a measure of knowledge about experience. The Afrocentric insists on steering the minds of readers and listeners in the direction of intellectual wholeness. (164)

A developing awareness of the black aesthetic requires a sensitivity to the cultural character of the rhetoric, the haunting communication styles of "epic memory," the racial ethos of the oral traditions which have survived through oppression (Asante 1987; Cobb 1985). If the despair from oppression becomes a dominant theme, it is not an aesthetic weakness because it contradicts the American ideal of optimism (Turner 1985).

"Nommo" and the Lyrical Attitude

Forbidden to learn to read or write, vocal communication becomes the central medium for the African in America; and "nommo," in African discourse "the generative and productive power of the spoken word," establishes the ancestral oral traditions on American soil.

The structural codes of lyrical quality, voice, and indirection present an Afro-American approach to language most consonant with narration. The public orator and the preacher employ these devices in their speeches, eliciting call-response patterns, "talk-backs," hand claps of affirmation. Examples from the orations of King, Brown, Jackson, and the like, as well as from characters drawn from the literary works of Baldwin, Wright, Jones, and the like, demonstrate these characteristics. Asante uses James Weldon Johnson's "The Creation" to illustrate these devices.

Indirection and Narrative Sequencing

Besides lyrical patterns and voice, "indirection" is used by speakers to arouse curiosity, suspense, and emotion. Building "deductively," the orator skillfully "stalks the issues," speaking circuitously, slowly leading up to the statement. Contrary to the Eurocentric approach, the use of indirection in this discourse tradition is valued as a test of rhetorical talent.

Narrative sequencing offers teachers an excellent method for making connections from the text to the audience. This strategy is the elaboration of the tale which links it to the lives of the listeners. Those of us who believe that we can link up great literary works with our students' prior knowledge can easily capitalize on this technique. In his discussion of the black folk sermon, Cook offers a number of good sources to use for this exercise.

Sudicism and Personalism

"In tune with the rhythm of the universe," says Asante, one who aspires to the sudic ideal moves in time with others—in the perpetual pursuit of *harmony*.

> There is no end to this challenge of becoming a person because there is no end to seeking harmony . . . you become more human as the master of your own powers, but always in the midst of others. (185–86)

Based on this sudicism, personalism involves the commitment to harmony within the person. This Afrocentric approach enables the person to become "the marker, the tagger for what is real." Thus, the Zulu causes his heart to stop for several minutes; the Asante or the Yoruba walks on fire without burning or plants a sword into the earth which cannot be removed; and this "activated energy" is understood as the sudic creation of "person."

An awareness of these principles allows us to understand better the legends and traditions of this culture where all that really matters is the person and his or her "oneness" with the other dimensions. Thus the symbols, the meanings of life, the place of the person with respect to the universe must be seen in a different perspective and must be appreciated differently in our literature.

Mythology

African-American mythology usually takes place in an indefinite time frame (unless it is historical, e.g., the story of Harriet Tubman) and relates the triumphs and victories of its heroes and heroines. The person, not nature, has control over the circumstances. It is the person's mission to overcome obstacles in the name of peace, love, and harmony. The mythological character "Shine" is portrayed as a symbol of hope and self-discovery in the face of chaos. Historical characters like Harriet Tubman and mythic figures like John Henry represent the individual meeting crisis with courage, challenge with strength (Asante 1987).

Stanford and Amin's chapter on black myth and legend is particularly helpful for use in the classroom.

Drama

> To exclude Afro-American playwrights from curricula leads to the erroneous conclusion that blacks have contributed little to the development of the American theater. . . . Afro-American drama . . . must be performed . . . presented as literature, as a viable teaching strategy, as a motivator for . . . self-concept . . . for oral interpretation . . . for attaining information and education about the Afro-American experience. (Robinson 1985, 315)

Illustrating classroom activities using such notable plays as Branch's *A Medal for Willie* and Peterson's *Take a Giant Step,* Robinson describes a number of teaching strategies from improving reading through reader's theatre to understanding one's own struggle and needs by improvisation and role-playing. Like the other literary genres, Afro-American drama must be part of mainstream curricula *and* treated in specially designated courses of study. Since there is often no distance between actors and audience in black American theatre (Asante 1987) and because the issues are both Afrocentric and universal, the study of drama becomes an important tool in teaching literature and one which has, heretofore, been limited.

Conclusion

Implicit in the teaching of English is the desire to show students the wisdom, the pleasures, and the comforts of literature, and the ability to express one's own feelings and ideas through the written and spoken word. Because we have been educated in a tradition which assumes exclusive rights, it is becoming more and more apparent that we are precluding a great many successful experiences for our students and ourselves. If we can take Molefi Asante's advice and extend our knowledge of the universe by adapting a worldview, we will be better able to value art forms of all cultures by understanding what makes them precious.

It is curious that the Eurocentric models from which we have long ago learned to judge have dominated western thought and value and "culture" and currently lay claim to possess "the stuff that cultural literacy is made of."

> Where we happen to be born, and when, largely determines the culture we acquire. The family, the neighborhood, the region, and

the nation can all make a difference. Initially, we have little control over the language we learn to speak, the concepts and stereotypes we acquire, the religion we accept, the gestures and expressions that amuse or reassure us, or the behavior that offends or pleases. Furthermore, we tend to assume that our way is the best way. (Bennett 1986, 8)

Because of our culture's xenophobic deficiencies, our system of education—our schools, our teachers, our curricula—lacks knowledge, and our students suffer as a result. In view of the rising dropout rates and the poor achievement of those who remain in school, we must act quickly and dramatically to expand our perceptions to include the world in its entirety and put all of its pieces back into the picture.

Works Cited

Asante, Molefi Kete. 1987. *The Afrocentric Idea.* Philadelphia: Temple UP.

Bennett, Christine I. 1986. *Comprehensive Multicultural Education: Theory and Practice.* Boston: Allyn.

Cobb, Martha K. 1985. "From Oral to Written: Origins of a Black Literary Tradition." *Tapping Potential: English and Language Arts for the Black Learner.* Ed. Charlotte K. Brooks. Urbana: NCTE.

Cook, William W. 1985. "The Afro-American Griot." *Tapping Potential: English and Language Arts for the Black Learner.* Ed. Charlotte K. Brooks. Urbana: NCTE.

Farr, Marcia, and Harvey Daniels. 1986. *Language Diversity and Writing Instruction.* Urbana: NCTE.

Hornburger, Jane. 1985. "Literature and Black Children." *Tapping Potential: English and Language Arts for the Black Learner.* Ed. Charlotte K. Brooks. Urbana: NCTE.

Kiah, Rosalie Black. 1985. "The Black Teenager in Young Adult Novels by Award-Winning Authors." *Tapping Potential: English and Language Arts for the Black Learner.* Ed. Charlotte K. Brooks. Urbana: NCTE.

Robinson, Edward A. 1985. "Afro-American Drama in Education: An Instructional Strategy." *Tapping Potential: English and Language Arts for the Black Learner.* Ed. Charlotte K. Brooks. Urbana: NCTE.

Smitherman-Donaldson, Geneva. 1987. "Toward a National Public Policy on Language." *College English* 49.1: 29–36.

Stanford, Barbara Dodds, and Karima Amin. 1978. *Black Literature for High School Students.* Urbana: NCTE.

Turner, Darwin T. 1985. "Black Experience, Black Literature, Black Students, and the English Classroom." *Tapping Potential: English and Language Arts for the Black Learner.* Ed. Charlotte K. Brooks. Urbana: NCTE.

From English Journal, *September 1988, 49–53*

12 "Old Man Coyote Makes the World": Using Native American Tales

Francis E. Kazemek, Muriel Radebaugh, and Pat Rigg

Who is Old Man Coyote? In Native American folklore, Coyote is many things:

> He made the Indians. . . . He gave all the people different names and taught them different languages. . . . He taught the people how to eat and how to hunt the buffalo and catch eagles. . . . He taught them how to dance. Sometimes he made mistakes, and even though he was wise and powerful, he did many foolish things. But that was his way.
>
> Coyote like to play tricks. . . . Sometimes he would go too far with some trick and get someone killed. . . . Another way he got in trouble was trying to do what someone else did. This is how he came to be called Imitator. . . . Coyote was ugly too. The girls did not like him. But he was smart. . . . Coyote got the girls when he wanted. (Lopez, 1977, pp. 179–80)

A Proviso

Coyote tales come from an oral tradition, and as such they are grounded in specific cultural contexts. We are not Native Americans; we do not come from cultures with long and continuous oral traditions. We are white, middle-class academics rooted deeply within a print culture. Because we are not Native Americans, we make no pretense that we understand Coyote tales as Native Americans do. As contemporary poet Gary Snyder says about his own reading of Coyote tales, "I'm only reading Coyote as I can, namely twentieth century, West Coast white American. How the Native American people themselves actually saw Coyote, actually used it, is another question . . ." (1977, p. 85). We do believe, however, that even with our limited understanding we can use Coyote tales for enjoyment and learning in the classroom.

Old Man Coyote

Erdoes and Ortiz (1984) contend that Coyote ultimately represents the primordial creativity that exists in all of us. Snyder (1977) says that Coyote is a symbol of the American West and reflects an interaction between *Myth* and a *Sense of Place*. At its greatest, the results of this creativity can be found in stories, poems, paintings, and music. However, Coyote also represents the elements that well up in all of us and lead to many imaginative creations that spring from all of us on a daily basis, creations of which we are usually unaware—jokes, metaphors, rhymes, witty asides, and variations to popular songs that we sing to ourselves. The important thing about Coyote, as Snyder (1977) observes, is that such creation is wedded to a particular place. Coyote reflects the Native Americans' creative spirit rooted in their dedication to and their love of the land.

Most importantly, we believe that Coyote is a symbol of psychological and moral complexity. He does not represent a simplistic dualism which attempts to separate the world into such dichotomies as *good* and *bad* or *black* and *white*. Coyote can be helpful, compassionate, intelligent and responsible; and, as Erdoes and Ortiz (1984) observe, at other times he is irresponsible, lecherous, a rebel, a breaker of taboos, an archetype of unrestrained spontaneity. Like the Oriental notion of yin and yang, Coyote symbolizes the integrally related capabilities for good and ill and for creation and stagnation inherent in all people. Coyote brought fire to humanity, but he also brought death into the world.

In sum, Coyote is like all of us. Like us in our worst moments, he is at times selfish and mean-spirited. Like us in our better moments, he is at times selfless and compassionate. Like us, Coyote is sometimes dull and plodding, but at other times he is inspired and creative. Like us, Coyote is both humorous and serious, both a braggart and self-effacing, both a generous gift-giver and a stingy hoarder. He is, like us, a contradiction.

Coyote and Early Adolescence

As a figure of moral and psychological complexity, Coyote is especially appropriate for the middle-school and junior high school classroom. Early adolescence is a time of complexity and change. Young people discover through abstract reasoning that the world is infinitely more complex and wonderful than they realized; blacks and whites merge into varying shades of gray. Likewise, young people begin to experience physiological and emotional changes that at times cause them to leap with joy in sweet, spontaneous growth while at other times causing them to despair over the strange and frightening things that are happening to them and over which they seem to have no control. And as they work with adults and each other in different situations, in various ways reflecting the ambiguous nature of reality, they form and test their own moral systems. And this developing sense of morality is highly complex in actual use.

Coyote not only represents the complexity and contradictions of the world but also, by his very nature, embodies the characteristics of young people. Indeed, Coyote is an excellent symbol for the young. He is energetic and can be both witty and dull, arrogant at one moment and painfully shy the next. Coyote is fun-loving, irreverent, crude, overtly sexual, irresponsible, and unpredictable. Anyone who has worked with junior high students knows that these characteristics equally describe seventh and eighth graders. Coyote is also capable of sensitivity, hard work, dedication, kindness, and selflessness, and, again, anyone who has seen junior high school kids work long and intently on a project which they as a whole group are excited about knows that these characteristics also describe seventh and eighth graders.

Thus, we believe that Coyote tales offer middle and junior high school teachers and students opportunities not only to explore the character of Coyote but also to explore a Native American view of the world. This view tends to be different and more complex and whole than that which we find in a Western European tradition. This *fuller* vision relates all things in the universe to one another, invests all things—both living and non-living—with some kind of awareness and worth, and offers opportunities for junior high students to explore their place in the world and their relationships to other people, animals, and things.

Coyote in the Classroom

We will briefly suggest five activities which use Coyote tales to promote cooperative language use in small group settings to make something with language.

Coyote Tales and Reading

Coyote tales can be a catalyst for reading other Coyote tales and Native American myths and legends (we list a few books for teachers and students in the bibliography). Because Coyote tales are usually short and fun to read, they allow even the most reluctant or inefficient readers to read successfully and to share what they've read. One easy way to do this is to have the students pair up and tell each other about what they've read. The value of students' talking to their classmates about their reading in relaxed situations cannot be underestimated. Retelling allows students not only to recall what they've read but to reflect upon it and to reorder it mentally, synthesizing what they understand from the reading with their own thoughts and feelings. And of course, paired retelling often stimulates students to read more books, because they want to read the story they've just heard retold by a friend.

As Lopez (1977) points out, Coyote tales may differ from tribe to tribe, but they all share certain universal characteristics. Thus, students can read, for example, different versions of how Coyote made humans and compare and contrast the various aspects of these tales. Such discussion and analysis allows students to develop not only a sense of story structure for particular kinds of tales but also allows them to focus on aspects of life that seem to be most important to Native Americans.

And, of course, Coyote tales should lead to reading and sharing other works about and by Native Americans (see Stensland, 1979). More universally, Coyote tales can serve as a bridge to tales from around the world. Students and teachers can explore the many guises in which the archetypal figure of trickster-imitator appears. Among Native Americans, the trickster appears as Raven, Hare, Badger, Bear, and Bluejay, among others. In Africa, he is Anansi the spider and Old Man Jackal. In Western Europe he is usually Fox and sometimes Wolf. Southern Black American folk tales have Brer Rabbit as the trickster character. And there are elements of the trickster in such human tall-tale figures as Mike Fink and Pecos Bill (who, by the way, was raised by a pack of coyotes). It is also fun to explore with students contemporary guises in which the trickster appears. Superhero comic books offer many possibilities here with such "flawed" superheroes as Hulk, Swampthing, Manthing, and so forth; all of these figures have the power to transform themselves in various ways and, like Coyote, possess both positive and negative characteristics.

Coyote Tales and Writing

Once students are familiar with the basic characteristics of Coyote and the structure of Coyote tales, they can create their own tales. At the beginning, such writing could be done as a whole-class project with the teacher taking an active role. Later, small groups can collaborate to create tales. Finally, students can create individual Coyote stories, exploring and expressing their own ideas about Coyote. With all these writing activities, teachers may want to use other items for discussion in addition to the Coyote tales themselves. "Roadrunner and Wiley Coyote" cartoons offer students an opportunity to discuss why and how the figure of Coyote has been perverted in the white mass media. Conversely, the wonderful Coyote paintings of contemporary artist Harry Fonseca can serve as a catalyst for examining why and how this artist has incorporated Coyote into his art and worldview.

Many Coyote tales are *why* tales which explore how something came to be; for example, "How Coyote Brought Fire to the People," "How Coyote Made Human Beings," and "How Coyote Got His Cunning." Such *why* or *pourquoi* tales are universal. Folklore and literature from around the world contain stories of how things came to be the way they are. Thus, Coyote tales can also lead to the writing of *why* tales about things in the students' everyday lives.

Coyote and Storytelling

Coyote tales come from an oral tradition; they were told for specific reasons in specific situations. One of the best ways for students to begin to get an idea of the richness of an oral tradition is to have them tell Coyote tales to one another in small groups and to younger students in other classrooms. If we want students to express themselves clearly with imagination, wit, intelligence, and conviction, then Coyote tales, either those students have read or written, offer excellent opportunities.

Similarly, students can tell their own or other *pourquoi* tales to peers or younger children. It is important for students to explore differences between spoken and written language and to understand they are not the same thing. Students who read, write, and tell *why* tales will recognize that different forms of language are not interchangeable and that each has its own special capacity and capabilities for expression.

Coyote and Creative Dramatics

One language activity too often absent from middle-school and junior high classrooms is creative dramatics. Students may occasionally perform plays which they have spent an inordinate amount of time rehearsing; but that activity does not allow for spontaneous—and regular—use of role taking, body movement, dialogue, and imaginative use of *found* props and the environment. Since Coyote tales are full of action and are also relatively short, they lend themselves well to dramatic interpretation. Students in small groups can read their own or other Coyote tales and prepare to perform the tale before their peers or students. Such re-visioning of a work from one language form to another not only allows students to see how one language mode relates to another but also fosters group cooperation and language collaboration in the classroom.

Coyote Tales and Singing

Native Americans use chants to tell their stories, something that even the most off-key singer can do. And since chanting is done as a group activity, it allows even shy or reticent students to participate in this form of poetry. Even students who hate poetry can come to enjoy it through participating in an oral performance involving volume, pitch, rhyme, and rhythm.

We suggest that, as with writing, chanting begin as a whole-class activity with the teacher playing an integral role. After reading a Coyote tale, the class can brainstorm elements of the story that seem to be most important. The class can then focus on lines that seem to best express those elements. With the teacher's help at first, the class can play around with ways to put together these lines into a rhythmical chant. After a little practice, the class can perform the chant for another class or group of younger children.

In one of the coyote tales about the creation of the world, Coyote is told by the Great Spirit to go out and begin his work. "Coyote was glad. He went right out and began his work. This is the way it was with him. He went out to make things right" (Lopez, 1977, p. 3). We hope that with the aid of Coyote tales, reading and language teachers can go out and make things *right* with their students by using materials and activities that are whole, worthwhile, and fun.

References

Baylor, Byrd. *And It Is Still That Way.* New York: Scribner, 1976.

de Wit, Dorothy (ed.). *The Talking Stone: An Anthology of Native American Tales and Legends.* New York: Greenwillow, 1979.

Erdoes, Richard and Alfonso Ortiz (eds.). *American Indian Myths and Legends.* New York: Pantheon, 1984.

Hayes, Joe. *Coyote and Native American Folk Tales Retold by Joe Hayes.* Mariposa Publishing, 1983.

Highwater, Jamake. *Anpao: An American Indian Odyssey.* (Especially "Anpao and Coyote: Farting Boy Tale," pp. 151–58). New York: Harper and Row, 1977.

Hodges, Margaret. *The Fire Bringer: A Paiute Indian Legend.* Boston: Little, Brown, 1972.

Jones, Hettie. *Coyote Tales.* New York: Holt, Rinehart, and Winston, 1974.

Lopez, Barry Holstun. *Giving Birth to Thunder, Sleeping with His Daughter; Coyote Builds North America.* Sheed Andres and McMeel, 1977.

Radin, Paul. *The Trickster: A Study in American Indian Mythology.* New York: Schocken, 1972.

Ramsey, Jarold (ed.). *Coyote Was Going There: Indian Literature of the Oregon Country.* Seattle: University of Washington Press, 1977.

Robinson, Gail A. and Douglas Hill. *Coyote the Trickster.* Crane Rursak, 1976.

Snyder, Gary. "The Incredible Survival of Coyote" in *The Old Ways: Six Essays by Gary Snyder.* San Francisco: City Lights Books, 1977.

Stensland, Anna Lee. *Literature by and about the American Indian: An Annotated Bibliography.* Urbana, Illinois: NCTE, 1979.

Thompson, Stith (ed.). *Tales of the North American Indians.* Bloomington: Indiana University Press, 1966.

From English Journal, *February 1987, 100–103*

13 Text and Context: Teaching Native American Literature

Diane Long Hoeveler

Silence is a major value in Native American culture, for silence is the token of acceptance, the symbol of peace and serenity, and the outward expression of harmony between the human and natural worlds. The result of this tradition of silence, however, is a limited written record, a limited number of texts produced by Native Americans themselves. This situation allowed the Anglo to step into the void and speak for Native Americans themselves, or more accurately, to claim to speak as their "interpreters." The implication that white culture drew from the lack of a written language in any of the Native American tribes was that these people had nothing of value to say to themselves or to others. It was not until the past twenty years that Native Americans have begun to produce their own literary works written in English with an eye toward communicating with the American population as a whole. Until the publication of Scott Momaday's *House Made of Dawn* (1968), the general population had not heard actual Native Americans speak in their own voices—the white culture had been speaking for them. During the past twenty years, however, there has been a veritable explosion of texts coming from the Native American community, and we now have a substantial corpus to use in teaching contemporary Native American literature.

The Unit: Themes for Reading and Writing

I teach contemporary Native American literature as a six-week unit in a secondary course entitled American Ethnic Literature. Although there are several anthologies of Native American literature, my choice as "best" for the high school student is *The American Indian Speaks* (Ed. John R. Milton, 1970, Vermillion, SD: U of South Dakota P). The major value of this anthology lies in its diversity of selections—poems, essays and short stories all written by Native Americans themselves.

There are also essays on Indian art, dance, and music, all of which give the student some necessary theoretical background on how Indian art differs from and must be evaluated by different criteria from white/ Anglo art. The other major strength of the collection stems from its contemporaneity—its works are written within the last twenty years and speak to the current situation of the Native American community; yet they retain their resemblance to the oral literary traditions of Native American tribal cultures.

I would not be perfectly honest about the experience of teaching Native American literature if I did not state that my students begin the course with negative stereotypes about "Indians" and extremely limited historical knowledge about the actual treatment of Native Americans in this country. Their attitudes and perceptions have been shaped by John Wayne movies, television programs, and a popular culture that has depicted the "Indians" as bloodthirsty savages who specialized in slaughtering innocent women and children. Rather than start with a lecture that debunks these attitudes, however, I let the literature speak for itself. What emerges from the first group of poems—written by Simon Ortiz, Norman H. Russell, and James Welch—is their over-whelming respect for nature as divine. This theme becomes the topic of the students' first essay. With this background firmly in place, then, it becomes much easier for students to understand the basic value conflict between the white and Native American cultures. They can see it spelled out in Frank Waters's essay "Two Views of Nature: White and Indian," and they can begin to understand how these two views set the stage for the disaster that was played out throughout the nineteenth century across the western plains.

The second idea we explore concerns the theme of survival as expressed in the literature. The corruption of traditional values and the assault on the Indian family are explored most forcefully and poignant-ly in "Woman Singing" by Simon Ortiz as well as in the poems of Ronald Rogers and Donna Whitewing. Students are asked to use these works to answer the following questions: What do today's Indians have to do to survive in a white-dominated culture? How has the "white man" corrupted Indian values and traditions? How do Indians feel about this situation? What are some of the contradictions between Indian traditions and the reality of life in contemporary America? At this point in the anthology and the course, students are often over-whelmed with a sense of pessimism and hopelessness at the plight of Indians in contemporary American society, which is why the next unit is a welcome relief and concludes the course on a more positive note.

The major emphasis of the last readings in the anthology and the topic of the last assigned essay focus on the power of Indian traditions, the value of the "old ways," and the relevance of Indian tribal practices and religious beliefs for the Native American today. Works such as "Day with Yaya," "The Turquoise Beads," "My Indian Name," "Clearing in the Valley," and "The Promised Visit" all develop a similar theme: how contemporary Indians can redeem their ethnic identity by preserving the ancient and sacred traditions of Native American culture. But preserving and defending this heritage is no easy task, and the poems at the conclusion of the anthology express some of the difficulties inherent in that effort. The displacement of the urbanized Indian is tragically expressed in Bruce Ignacio's "Lost," while the isolation and friendlessness of the Indian find utterance in Loyal Shegonee's "Loneliness" and Rosey Garcia's "Then and Now." Kay C. Bennett makes the point that Native Americans somehow, miraculously, have managed to survive and preserve their traditions on the reservation, but that the ultimate white weapon against Indian culture—welfare—may succeed finally in wiping out the last vestiges of that carefully nurtured life (see her "Letter to the Editor," Milton 171-72). The challenge confronting Native Americans today is not really significantly different from what it has been since the mid-1800s. Preserving one's dignity and heritage has been the challenge of every ethnic group in America. The tragic fact is that the Indians—like the European Jews—have had to survive a virtual attempt at genocide in the process of preserving their traditions. And all of this to a large extent can be traced to bifurcated perceptions of the land as sacred or the land as commodity. That basic dichotomy between Indian and white values underlies and to a large extent precipitated the crisis and the continuing dilemma.

Individual Projects

I assign one individual project that requires the students to read one author in depth or research a topic in Indian history, art, music, or culture. The assignment of this project has produced some amazing results, for in the very act of researching one topic in depth the students uncover more than they could ever discover within the confines of the classroom. One particularly insightful project was on Indian food as symbol in literature and life, with supplementary demonstrations and tastings in class. Another interesting project was an analysis of Indian legends and mythologies, with demonstrations on symbols in Indian blankets, pottery, and sand paintings (purchased by the student's family on vacations to New Mexico). Students have also scheduled a film such as "North American Indian Legends" (1973, Phoenix Films; also available in videotape) as a visual accompaniment to their oral presentations. This film, featuring the original legends of Indians in three different geographical regions, provides an effective illustration of how legends express both cultural and spiritual values as well as explanations of natural events. Another student, a virtual expert on contemporary music, presented an extremely informative discussion of current popular music by Native Americans. He started with Buffy Sainte-Marie but went much beyond her in analyzing the themes and concerns of Indian protest music today. Other students chose one particular tribe and researched the life, language, food, clothing, and religious and oral traditions unique to that group. The students focused on how the geographical surroundings influenced the tribe's adaptation and traditions, then presented their findings in a panel discussion in which each student was an "expert" on that particular tribe.

Finally, several students chose to read works by major contemporary Native Americans writing today—James Welch, Vine Deloria, N. Scott Momaday, Leslie Silko, and Patty Harjo. Novels like *Winter in the Blood, The Death of Jim Loney, House Made of Dawn,* and *Ceremony* all hold a strong appeal for my students. The alienation in these novels speaks directly to the alienation that these adolescents feel, and they identify strongly with the protagonists of these works. The major lesson they learn, however, is that contemporary Native American literature has to be read as imaginative art in its own right, and that it can be evaluated ultimately by the standards applied to all literature. When they write about their personal and tribal experiences, Native Americans are creating imagistic and symbolic worlds, literary visions of truth, not simply political, historical, or sociological tracts. As their final exam in the course, students write on the universal themes developed in Native American literature. They have come to realize that we are all strangers, outsiders within a culture that we all experience as alien to ourselves. In identifying with the Indian dilemma, my students learn that we all share basic human emotions and needs for a life of dignity, harmony, peace, and acceptance.

Resources

The other crucial resources that enrich the educational experience of my students are audiovisual materials, field trips, and guest lecturers. I will outline here some of the larger themes these resources develop and suggest when and how they would be appropriate to use. Our initial focus is on the characteristics and specific history of Native American literature, and in conjunction with this theme I show the two-part filmstrip "American Indian Literature" (1980, Films for the Humanities). These filmstrips contrast the usual white view of the Indians to the more recent depiction presented by Native Americans themselves. I distribute a worksheet I have made to accompany this filmstrip and ask the students to list in parallel columns the stereotypes about Indians that white culture has propagated in contrast to the way Indians view themselves. This initial exercise helps the students to formulate the differences between white and Indian values, while at the same time it forces them to understand the role whites have played in distorting the image of the Indian. Another two-part filmstrip that can be used in identical fashion is "We Are Indians: American Indian Literature" (1973, Guidance Associates). This filmstrip presents traditional Indian values and symbols on the first tape and shows their desecration by white society on the second tape.

The second theme we address in the unit is the history of Manifest Destiny and its role in altering the Indians' way of life. Students are generally familiar with this idea from their American history course, but in this class we look at Manifest Destiny from the Indians' perspective, which, of course, changes everything. I begin by showing "The North American Indian: Treaties Made, Treaties Broken" (film and videotape, 1970, CRM Films), which explores in depth the history of one treaty: the 1854 Treaty of Medicine Creek signed by the Indians of Washington state. The second film that continues the historical saga is entitled "The North American Indian: How the West Was Won and Honor Lost" (film and videotape, 1970, CRM Films), using paintings, newspaper accounts, and photographs to tell the story of the breaking of treaties, the removal of the Indians from the land, and the Trail of Tears. Two other films that contrast with each other are "Custer: The American Surge Westward" (1965, McGraw-Hill) and "I Will Fight No More Forever: The Story of Chief Joseph" (1975, McGraw-Hill). In these two films we see an important contrast in leadership styles as well as another version of the white/Indian value conflict. Another film which depicts the history of the white and Indian conflict in a very personal way is *Little Big Man* (available on videotape), starring Dustin Hoffman. Students particularly enjoy this film and often choose to read the book by Thomas Berger on which the film is based. The final film in the historical series, entitled "The North American Indian: Lament of the Reservation" (1970, McGraw-Hill), is narrated by Marlon Brando and powerfully depicts the results of Manifest Destiny: we see what it is like to live on a Sioux reservation in South Dakota today. The suicide rate among young Sioux teenagers is particularly tragic and conveys to my students the desperation of the young Indian in a direct and effective manner.

The films on Indian history lend themselves to a number of interesting activities. Students enjoy going to the library and using the microfilmed collection of the *New York Times* to see how that newspaper presented the events that led, for instance, to the 1877 conflict between the US Army and the Nez Perces. I have also assigned journal writings in which students take the role of an Indian or white eyewitness to a battle or treaty meeting. Keeping an imaginary diary or writing letters to a friend in the East requires students to project themselves into the past and identify with distant historical events.

The next theme we develop is the struggle for survival and the role legends and myths have played in keeping Indian traditions alive. To supplement this unit I show "The American Indian Speaks" (videotape, 1973, Encyclopaedia Britannica), which illustrates several viewpoints on the struggle for survival while vividly depicting scenes of contemporary Indian life and problems. A videotape which nicely complements this theme is entitled "Hopi Songs of the Fourth World," a 58-minute color exploration of life on the major Hopi reservations today (film and videotape, Ferrero/New Day Films; also available as a 30-minute videotape). This film provides a detailed examination of the food, living conditions, tribal rituals, and art of the Hopi tribe. Indians have always turned to their culture and legends to understand their lives, and to demonstrate how this is still done I show "American Indians: Yesterday and Today" (1981, Filmfair Communications). In this film spokesmen and women from their distinctly different tribes tell the stories of their people and explain how their religious beliefs have enabled them to persevere in the face of tremendous oppression. To make this unit more immediate to my students I construct an analogous situation for them. I ask them to imagine and then write about what their lives would be like if we were invaded by an alien race with a radically different culture, religion, language, and government. Students often choose to imagine an extraterrestrial alien invasion or one by the Russians, and they depict themselves clinging to their "old ways" as the only means they have of maintaining their original identities.

The final audiovisual unit I plan utilized the recent film *The Emerald Forest*, available on videotape. This extremely powerful film shows that white culture is now desecrating and exterminating the Indian tribes of South America, specifically those which have lived in harmony with nature for thousands of years in Brazil. In this film a young white boy, son of an American engineer, is kidnapped by an Indian tribe and raised as the son of the tribe's chief. After years of searching, the father finds his son, but the boy, now considered by the Indians to be a man, has no wish to return to white society. In fact, at film's end he is made chief of his tribe upon the death of the Indian father. This brief summary of the film cannot do justice to its beauty, complexity, or the power it exerts over its viewers. Showing the film is a very effective way to conclude the course, for *The Emerald Forest* makes clear that the policy of Manifest Destiny continues today, displacing the Indians of South America, the latest victims of greed and the commercialization of nature. The film always elicits lively class discussion and debate, and one technique I have found successful is to have students role-play either the father or son, or to take turns debating pro or con positions on the basic question: is it justifiable to destroy the Brazilian rain forest in order to build roads, villages, and dams in the name of "civilization"?

The final resource I have used to bring the course alive for my students is to plan field trips and to bring in guest speakers, neither of which I realize may be possible in every geographical locale. I have taken students to Chicago's Natural History Museum, which houses one of the world's largest collections of Indian artifacts and displays. Entire villages from various geographical settings are reconstructed here, and experts are available to lead the students through the entire wing. Visits have also been scheduled to the Indian collection at Milwaukee's Public Museum, particularly when a special touring exhibit on Indian art was available. Guest speakers have also been invited from the local Indian Cultural Center. I specifically want to contrast the museum displays, which tend to put the Indian under glass as a dead object, to the living guest speaker, who lets the students know that Indians are alive and struggling to preserve their culture and values in the midst of an urban environment.

Teaching Native American literature has been as much a positive growth experience for me as a teacher as I know it has been for my students. We are no longer trying to speak for the Native Americans; we are simply letting ourselves hear them. We are humbled and shamed by the story they tell of their history, but we are also inspired by the vision of nature they still tenaciously possess. We are involved in their struggle, if only in being better informed.

Sources for Films Cited

Britannica Training and Development, Britannica Center, 310 S. Michigan Ave., 6th Floor, Chicago, IL 60604. (800) 554-9862, or in Illinois, (312) 347-7400

CRM Films, 2233 Faraday Ave., Suite F, Carlsbad, CA 92008. (619) 431-9800

Ferrero/New Day Films, 121 West 27th St., No. 902, New York, NY 10001. (212) 645-8210

Filmfair, 10621 Magnolia Blvd., North Hollywood, CA 91601. (818) 985-0244

Films for the Humanities, P.O. Box 2053, Princeton, NJ 08540. (800) 257-5126

Guidance Associates, Communications Park, Box 3000, Mt. Kisco, NY 10549. (800) 431-1242

McGraw-Hill films cited in this article are no longer available.

Phoenix Films, 468 Park Avenue South, New York, NY 10016 (212) 684-5910

Background Reading

One cannot simply teach Native American literature as if the genre began in 1968. If you are like most traditionally trained English teachers, you are probably not conversant with Native American literature; I know I was not. Approaching the field in order to teach it can be a daunting prospect, simply because there is a wealth of fairly specialized material that is quite foreign to the average English teacher. Anyone preparing to teach a course or unit on Native American literature should begin with a careful reading of a few very helpful studies that provide valuable background for teachers: Paula Gunn Allen's *Studies in American Indian Literature: Critical Essays and Course Designs* (1983, MLA), Abraham Chapman's *Literature of the American Indians: Views and Interpretations* (1975, NAL), and Brian Swann's *Smoothing the Ground: Essays on Native American Oral Literature* (1983, U of California P).

Once one is confident about one's own preparation, then one must begin by providing students with the necessary background to the field, and this is only gained by studying the traditional Indian oral narratives, the oratory and oral poetry, and the first works by Indians done during the nineteenth and early twentieth centuries. An overview for students can best be provided by using any one of several valuable texts or anthologies of Indian literature including Margot Atrov's *American Indian Prose and Poetry* (1962, Capricorn), John Bierhost, *In the Trail of the Wind* (1971, Farrar), Natalie Curtis, *The Indians' Book* (1968, Dover), and Dennis Tedlock, *Finding the Center* (1972, Dial). In the case of the oral narratives and poetry, one has to point out to students that these works have survived only because whites, primarily anthropologists, went out into the field and transcribed the cosmologies and poems. One has to realize, also, that most Indian writings produced before 1968 are what is known as "told-to" autobiographies. Those Indians who did write themselves were almost solely converts to Christianity, products of Christian educations, writing for the explicit purpose of converting other Indians.

Myth and legend are the other major areas of Indian tradition with which students should be familiar before they begin a study of contemporary literature. The best introductions to Indian mythologies can be found in Andrew Wiget's *Native American Literature* (1985, Twayne) and his *Critical Essays on Native American Literature* (1985, G. K. Hall). His works provide the historical, religious, and cultural background that students need to set the contemporary works in the fullest possible context. By analyzing the origin myths, legends, and oral traditions as fully as possible, students will be able to see the vital continuum that exists between past and present versions of Indian writing.

From English Journal, *September 1988, 20–24*